# The Children's Character Building Collection

## *Study Guide*

Grace and Truth Books

The Children's Character Building Collection Study Guide
ISBN # 978-1-960297-20-4

Published by Grace and Truth Books, 2025

Cover design by Roger Farrell
Drawings on pages 11, 43, 63, 118, 141 by Caffy Whitney
Interior layout by Sarah Lee Photo & Design

**Grace and Truth Books**
Phone: 501.459.5601
www.graceandtruthbooks.com

# Table of Contents

# HOW TO USE THIS STUDY GUIDE

We are enthused to finally present to you, this Study Guide for the eleven beloved children's stories from the 1800s which have been the heart of our company's product line for nearly three decades! We are certain this Study Guide will render the stories more useful and profitable to families than ever, providing a good selection of questions and answers as well as memory verses and suggested activities for each book.

In these eleven books of the Children's Character Building Collection, you will notice that, whenever the books quote a Bible verse, it is from King James Version. That was the only English version being widely used at the time these stories were written.

To assist families using this Discussion & Study Guide, we are going to list the Scriptures for you in two versions: The King James Version (KJV) and The English Standard Version (ESV).

A parent and child may use this guide in any manner that works well for you! But what we had in mind and suggest is: After a parent and child read a book chapter together, then talk through the questions together. This should normally be doable in about 20 minutes, but of course you can carry on the discussion for as long as you both find it enjoyable and beneficial!

Some questions are intended just for personal reflection and conversation. Others have a specific answer, and in those instances, the answer will be found in the Answers Section which is a mere turn of the page away.

Our study guide is not meant merely as a test or quiz, to make sure the reader is learning from the story; nor is it all just questions for study. Some of it is designed to simply make the story enjoyable and memorable to both the parent and student, and to provide you some worthy topics to explore and talk about together.

# THE BIBLE IN THE WALL
## Study Guide

Antonio is given a Bible, but he doesn't want this gift! He is annoyed, even resentful of it, due to irrational fears about the Bible, because he has been exposed to false teachings. But he finds a creative way to get rid of the disturbing gift. Still, our powerful and gracious God desires people to have His Word, and by His sovereign control over all events brings the Bible back to Antonio and transforms his life through it.

# Chapter 1:
# ANTONIO AND HIS BIBLE

1   The story begins in the year 1856. Talk about what was happening in the United States at that time (or whatever your country of residence, or world history) so you can picture this story in timeline and perspective. If you have a historical timeline, such as the Adams Chart of World History, this would be a good time to refer to it.

2   Has anyone ever given you a Bible? How did you react to that?

3   Antonio was very reluctant to accept this gift. He was even suspicious and resentful. What an odd reaction! What could have made him feel this way?

   Antonio is not the only person who ever got hostile when a Bible was brought around! Others do too, even today – but usually for different reasons. What are some of those reasons?

4   Here are some better and more Biblical attitudes about the Word of God:

   Psalm 119:162: "I rejoice at Your Word like one who finds great spoil." (ESV)

   "I rejoice at Thy word, as one that findeth great spoil." (KJV)

   Psalm 1:1-2: "Blessed is the man who does not walk in the counsel of the wicked, nor stands in the way of sinners, nor sits in the seat of scoffers; but his delight is in the law of the Lord, and on His law he meditates day and night." (ESV)

   "Blessed is the man that walketh not in the counsel of the ungodly, nor standeth in the way of sinners, nor sitteth in the seat of the scornful. But his delight is in the law of the Lord; and in his law doth he meditate day and night." (KJV)

   1 Peter 2:1-3: "So put away all malice and all deceit and hypocrisy and envy and all slander. Like newborn infants, long for the pure spiritual milk, that by it you may grow up into salvation – if indeed you have tasted that the Lord is good." (ESV)

   "Wherefore laying aside all malice, and all guile, and hypocrisies, and envies, and all evil speaking, as newborn babes, desire the sincere milk of the word, that ye may grow thereby: if so be ye have tasted that the Lord is gracious." (KJV)

5   We suggest you look up resources about Martin Luther and learn about him. Many people, when they hear this name, think instead of Dr. Martin Luther King (1929-1968)! But these are two very different people. Martin Luther was a German monk, then preacher and reformer in the 1500s (16th century). Make sure your child understands that these are two different people!

*Note: Not all questions or points have an answer provided here, as some of them were just raised for you to discuss with your child, or to get his reaction to the events in the story.*

1  If you have a historical timeline, such as the Adams Chart of World History, this would be a good time to refer to it (http://www.graceandtruthbooks.com/product/adams-syn-chronological-chart-and-map-of-history). In 1856, James Buchanan was elected President of the United States. He was the last one before Abraham Lincoln. The United States was in a time of serious tensions between north and south, over several issues, black slavery being one. John Brown led a massacre of men in Kansas in which many who opposed slavery were killed in a night; and even on the floor of the U.S. Senate, two Senators (Preston Brooks and Charles Sumner) had a fight over it, and Sen. Brooks ended up beating Sen. Sumner with his cane! Also, a little town began in Texas – named Dallas.

2  Just enjoy some conversation together on this question!

3  In Europe at that time, the Roman Catholic Church was teaching people that they should not even read the Bible, saying it was dangerous for them to do so, because it was too spiritual for them, "over their heads," and they should rely on the priests to tell them what it meant rather than read it for themselves. This was a serious error which, happily, we rarely hear anymore. While many despise the Bible today, at least pretty much everyone who goes to church at least believes that we should read it and learn from it ourselves, and not just wait for "experts" to tell us what it means!

Others will say, all the Bible does is make them feel guilty (sometimes, they should feel guilty!). Or, they may think that those who quote it to them are trying to make them feel condemned, using it to control them and not allow them to do what they want. We should always be gracious when we quote the Bible to people, and not use it to "smack down" people with a final answer on a subject, but be humble about it, as recipients of the grace of God ourselves. We also should not just make the Bible sound like a book full of rules and commandments, because it's so much more than that! It's the Story of the wondrous things God has done in the world!

What does the person who mocks the Bible need to happen in their heart? He or she needs a new heart, bestowed by the Holy Spirit, which receives and loves the Word of God. This does not come to people naturally but is a work of God in us. See Ezekiel 36:26-27 and Acts 16:14. The Lord is the one who opens hearts and changes hearts!

This is a worthy subject to talk at some length with your child about: How could people get to where they feel such an animosity to the Bible, even mocking it (as Antonio's co-workers did)? Ask your child if he knows anyone like that. What does the person who mocks the Bible need to happen in their heart?

4  No "answer" is provided here.

5  Here is a brief biography of Martin Luther: http://www.biography.com/people/martin-luther-9389283#later-years. We also highly recommend these books available from Grace and Truth Books:

  · *When Lightning Struck! The Story of Martin Luther*, by Danika Cooley (for children 8 to 12)
  · *What Should I Do? The True Story of Martin Luther and the Reformation*, by Catherine Mackenzie (for children ages 5 to 7)

# Chapter 2: THE WILD SOUTH WIND
# Chapter 3: THE FIRE

*It is best to read and discuss chapters 2 and 3 together; partly because chapter 2 is so brief, and also because they are really just aspects of the same incident.*

1. Find the town of Glarus, on a map of Switzerland or Google Earth. You are going to find a beautiful place! Have you ever seen mountains this big? The two mountains named in this chapter (Mt. Shilt and Mt. Glarnisch) are both nearly 10,000 feet in elevation! Besides Mt. Shilt and Mt. Glarnisch, there are many mountains in that region (known as The Alps) much bigger than those! Switzerland is an amazing land and enjoyable to learn and talk about; even moreso to visit!

2. Have you heard stories of other cities that were burned down by great fires?

3. Telegraphs (page 11) are certainly a thing of the past. Tell your child a bit of how this was the email or text messaging of two or three centuries ago!

4. For many centuries there have been volunteer fire departments, and there are even today. Does your family know a fireman? Why would men risk their lives for others, as volunteers (without pay)?

5. Why does the story bring up thankfulness (page 12) here? Was it sin that the villagers never thanked God for years and years of safety?

6. Despite failing to thank God, the citizens of Glarus did have this good trait: after the fire, in those needy, crisis days, they showed real, practical care for one another, being generous with food, shelter, construction, and helping one another rebuild. Has your family ever participated personally in disaster relief?

## Memory Verse
### Amos 3:6

"Does disaster come to a city, unless the Lord has done it?" (ESV)

"Shall there be evil in a city, and the Lord hath not done it?" (KJV)

1   Just enjoy talking about Switzerland and the mountains, beholding the beauty!

2   Tell a little about the stories of Chicago, and Rome, for instance. You may find others. There may even be some history of terrible, destructive fires in your own city or town. Here are some links about the famous fires in Chicago and Rome:

- http://www.history.com/topics/great-chicago-fire

- http://www.history.com/this-day-in-history/neros-rome-burns

Talk with your children about why the strong winds worried the people so much; this always makes destruction by fire much more likely and worse. This may not make sense to a child unless they understand how strong winds can spread fire. Explain how fire in a city can move from house to house, with embers carried in the wind. I was told by someone in Mexico once that, most homes are built with concrete walls and metal roofs, instead of wood, to make fire damage less likely.

3   Just enjoy the discussion on this one.

4   Explain how the work of volunteer firemen shows love for the people of their community. You can compare this to the love found in the gospel: Romans 5:6-8 – which is, of course, a far greater love. It is this love of God in Christ which, of course, we as the readers – and Antonio in the story – will learn more about later in this story.

5   Yes, it is in fact unthankful to enjoy safety and protection for years, and not thank God for it. After that is understood, consider raising this topic with your children: Is God at all obliged to protect people from danger, who never worship or serve Him, or thank Him? Certainly not.

6   Parents: Is there an opportunity near you to get in on this kind of relief effort – to help people, after damage from a flood, fire, tornado, hurricane or some other disaster? Consider doing so! Maybe there isn't right this moment; but when the need arises, consider how you can turn that into an educational moment while being a blessing to others too!

# Chapter 4:
# FINDING THE BIBLE

1. A new character emerges in our story: Mario. Talk about what Mario has learned (page 14) about "the deadly error of teaching salvation by works." What does this mean? Why is it deadly?

2. The word "doctrine" appears near the top of page 15. Many Christians feel an aversion to talking about doctrine. But is this the right attitude?

3. Giovanni loved his Bible but unfortunately, due to Catholic beliefs of those times, he was pressured to give it up. Do you love the Word of God? If you do, how will that show?

4. Have you ever read the Bible aloud to other people? This is a great method of evangelism. Especially when you don't know what to say to someone or how to witness to them, you can ask them if the two of you could just read the Bible together.

5. How do we learn to pray by reading the Psalms? (page 19)

6. The writer refers to "the blessings of being hated" (page 20). Now, that's a very unusual way to think! Nobody wants to be hated. What possible blessing could there be in being hated?

## Memory Verse

### Ephesians 2:8-9

"For by grace you have been saved through faith. And this is not your own doing; it is the gift of God, not a result of works, so that no one may boast." (ESV)

"For it is by grace you have been saved, through faith—and this is not from yourselves, it is the gift of God—not by works, so that no one can boast." (KJV)

1   The author means, it is fatal to a person's soul when he trusts in works for salvation. For there is no way to know God or the path to eternal life by our good works. If there is anything the Bible is clear about, it's this!

2   See Acts 2:42: the new converts to Christ in the first church ever are described there as devoted to four things, and one of them was "devoting themselves to the Apostle's doctrine." Explain to your child that the word doctrine just means teaching. Do we crave being taught about God? Of course we should, and hopefully we do! That is what doctrine means.

3   Love for the Word of God will show, of course, first of all by:

- Reading it with interest, a genuine desire to learn what God has to say.

- A habit of meditation on it (see Psalm 1). "Meditation" means, to not quickly forget what we have read, but to turn it over in one's mind, think about it often.

- A readiness to do what the Word says (see James 1:22-26)

4   A valuable book for making the most of this idea is *One to One Bible Reading*, by Paul Helm.

5   We often prove how true Romans 8:26 is, that we do not know how to pray. Reading Psalms gives us wonderful samples of men praising and worshiping God; confessing sin to God; making their requests to Him, and more. When you fail to find words to pray in, it is often a big help to pray with one of the Psalms!

For example: When you need to confess sin to God, try using Psalm 32 or Psalm 51 in your prayer. Or, if you want to worship God and can't think of the words to say, try declaring the words of one of these Psalms: 145 through 150.

6   Help your child grasp this biblical viewpoint. In Acts 5:41, after the Apostles had been arrested and beaten for preaching about Jesus, they considered it a joyful privilege that they were given the opportunity to suffer for the name of Jesus!

Also see Matthew 5:11-12: Jesus declares that we are blessed if we are spoken against and persecuted, because it shows who we really are!

Look also at John 15:18 to see that, when the world hates us, Jesus said to remember that they hated Him also. If walking close to Him results in us being hated, so be it. We will be far happier in the long run to have His favor than the world's!

# Chapter 5:
# GIOVANNI AND THE PRIEST

Notice, the story has now reached 1862. This is the timing of the middle of the Civil War in the USA. This may help your child place this story in history.

1  What is "the Latin mass"? (page 23)

2  How do you "hunger and thirst after righteousness"? (page 24) How is hungering and thirsting after righteousness different from being a person who just tries to do the right things?

3  Why were the Roman Catholic priests in Italy so opposed to ordinary people having a Bible of their own?

## Memory Verse
### 1 Peter 3:18

"For Christ also suffered once for sins, the righteous for the unrighteous, that He might bring us to God." (ESV)

"For Christ also hath once suffered for sins, the just for the unjust, that He might bring us to God." (KJV)

1  There are three huge problems with this Roman Catholic ceremony, which to a Protestant may appear to merely resemble the Lord's Supper. But it is not:

First, the Catholic Church believes that the bread turns literally into the body of Jesus Christ, and the juice turns into the literal blood of Jesus, when they pray over it.

Second, they also believe that during the ceremony, Jesus is being sacrificed again. This completely violates the biblical emphasis that Jesus Christ was sacrificed once for all, and that this act of His death for sinners will never be repeated. For the Son of God to die once was sufficient to pay for the sins of a world of sinners! He is never sacrificed again.

Third, they perform this ceremony in Latin because they believe that it is safer for the congregation to not hear the words about the death of Jesus in their own language, since, they say, the people are not trained to rightly interpret the words of the Bible. So they purposefully keep the language obscure so that only the priest knows what is being said and the people do not.

2  Remember that it is Jesus who said, people who do hunger and thirst after righteousness are blessed – they will be filled or satisfied (Matthew 5:6). That is, God will be pleased to give them that which they crave!

The difference between hungering and thirsting after righteousness, compared to just trying to do right, is the person who hungers and thirsts after it is more eager and serious about righteous living. He won't stop even when it becomes inconvenient, crossing his other desires, or when other people resist him and suggest temptations instead. He will press on in pursuit of righteousness because he truly craves or yearns for it.

3  We know this ground has been covered before, but it's a big theme in the story and so make sure it is understood. This resistance to ordinary people reading the Bible was because, the Roman Catholic church was trying to control people by insisting that only priests can correctly understand the Word of God. If they allowed the people to believe that they can understand the Scriptures themselves, it would be a possible obstacle to submission to the priests. In the U.S.A., not many Catholic churches are like this anymore; but it is still common among Catholic priests in other countries, especially in South America and Central America.

# Chapter 6:
# THE BIBLE STALL

Italy has come up a few times in the story now. Find the nation of Italy on a map of Europe.

1    The Bible colporteurs come up in this chapter. Doesn't this sound like a great way to spend your life or to make your living?! But – why would we sell people a copy of the Bible? Wouldn't it be better if we just gave a Bible to everyone?

2    This (page 28) is a good time to emphasize to your child that this is known to be a true story, and that God really did work in this way, causing the hidden Bible to be rediscovered and bring blessing to many.

3    Believers who seek to spread the Word of God have often been persecuted by others, and still are today. There are more than enough opportunities in today's news (especially when reading of Middle Eastern nations) to explain how this is happening in our times. Introduce your child to Voice of the Martyrs (www.vom.org)

## Memory Verse
### Matthew 5:11-12

"Blessed are you when others revile you and persecute you and utter all kinds of evil against you falsely on my account. Rejoice and be glad, for your reward is great in heaven, for so they persecuted the prophets who were before you." (ESV)

"Blessed are you when people insult you, persecute you and falsely say all kinds of evil against you because of me. Rejoice and be glad, because great is your reward in heaven, for in the same way they persecuted the prophets who were before you." (KJV)

1   Read about some of the history of men who made a living as Bible colporteurs here: http://en.wikipedia.org/wiki/Colportage

One possible reason they sold Bibles is, people who buy something – even for a small price – are more likely to read it, because they are interested. People who are given a Bible might not care enough about it to read it. So of course, giving Bibles is a fine thing to do, but colporteurs who sold it should not be looked down on, as they had a good idea which resulted in a lot of Bibles being distributed, and taken seriously by the readers who bought one.

On YouTube, search for Mary Jones and Her Bible and you'll find a wonderful, animated video (only 5 minutes long) of her true story, which illustrates this point memorably and beautifully.

2   Just enjoy the discussion on this point!

3   We cannot emphasize enough, introducing your child to Voice of the Martyrs is a great place to start.

# Chapter 7:
# ANTONIO IN THE HOSPITAL

1  What does Jesus mean in the verse (Revelation 3:20) quoted near the start of this chapter, about how He will "come in and sup with" someone who welcomes Him into their life? (by the way, "sup with" means "eat with" – as in, have supper with them)

2  What does "God's chastening hand" mean? Read Hebrews chapter 12 to learn about it, as Antonio did. Especially verses 5-6:

"And have you forgotten the exhortation that addresses you as sons? 'My son, do not regard lightly the discipline of the Lord, nor be weary when reproved by him. For the Lord disciplines the one he loves, and chastises every son whom he receives.'" (ESV)

Have you ever felt that you were being chastened by the Lord? Talk about this together.

3  According to this chapter, what is one of the most effective ways to see more missionaries raised up to go out into the world with the gospel? (page 33)

4  What is the meaning of "the publican's prayer" (page 36)?

## Memory Verse
### Matthew 9:38

"Pray earnestly to the Lord of the harvest, to send out laborers into His harvest." (ESV)

"Pray ye therefore the Lord of the harvest, that He will send forth labourers into His harvest." (KJV)

1   In ancient culture, being willing to share a meal with someone showed real friendship and care. It's not so different today. People who don't like each other don't usually want to eat together! But inviting someone to share a meal with you shows that you both like them and welcome their companionship. Jesus is using this cultural idea to show, we can have His fellowship and nearness, if we will come to Him.

2   Because God has all wisdom and Almighty power, He is able and willing to bring trouble and pain into our lives, if it is necessary to get us to see and do the right thing. He does this from love! Sometimes God will chasten His own people (Christians) to turn us from sin and get us to repent and change. He will also chasten unsaved people at times to get their attention and to draw them away from sin to Himself.

3   To pray! The lost people of the world are here described in a double illustration: as sheep without a shepherd and as a harvest ready to be brought in. This comes from Jesus' words and His command to pray for workers for the harvest, in Matthew 9:35-38.

4   A publican is an old word that the King James Version uses for people we now call tax collectors. The Bible tells a story about a publican in Luke 18:9-14 – read that wonderful story and look closely at his prayer. Be sure to talk about how the two men prayed in that Biblical story and observe the striking differences in their prayers.

Many Americans do not like or trust the IRS (Internal Revenue Service) today — and some of them have good reasons to feel that way! Some of the practices of IRS agents in recent years have been to target Christian organizations and try to punish them for their biblical beliefs. But in the times of Jesus, the tax collectors were worse! They were traitors to their nation Israel, who collected taxes from the Jewish people to pay Rome, which should never have been done. So Jews hated tax collectors and they believed every one of them was going to hell! But Jesus' words are meant to show us that even the worst kinds of sinners can still cry out to Him for mercy and grace, and be saved and forgiven! No one is so bad that they are beyond mercy. But if we praise ourselves for being righteous, that is a far greater danger than even having a lot of sin that needs forgiving!

# Chapter 8:
# CONCLUSION

1   What are the most important things you have learned from this story?

2   Why does the author say we cannot please God with outward forms and useless ceremonies?

3   The story of *The Bible in the Wall* closes by quoting Scriptures from Hebrews 10:24-25 and John 4:23-24. Why are these verses a perfect way to end the story?

## Memory Verse Options
### Hebrews 10:24-25

"And let us consider how to stir up one another to love and good works, not neglecting to meet together, as is the habit of some, but encouraging one another, and all the more as you see the Day drawing near." (ESV)

"And let us consider one another to provoke unto love and to good works: not forsaking the assembling of ourselves together, as the manner of some is; but exhorting one another: and so much the more, as ye see the day approaching." (KJV)

### John 4:24

"God is Spirit, and those who worship Him must worship in spirit and truth." (ESV)

"God is a Spirit: and they that worship Him must worship Him in spirit and in truth." (KJV)

1   There is a lot in this story about the preciousness of the Bible! It shows not only that we can be saved as we trust the truths about Christ that it reveals, but also shows how the Word of God guards us from false teachings. Share with your child how getting to know the Bible well will make them able to recognize wrong religious ideas, and make them able to help others to spot wrong teaching for what it is, too.

2   There are outward forms and ceremonies the Lord wants His church to do, such as baptism and taking the Lord's Supper. But we must not rely on these acts as if they will save us. We only do them in obedience to the Lord, after we are saved by His grace and forgiveness. We do not earn any "points" with God by doing these things.

3   Consider having your child write out his thoughts on why these verses are an appropriate way to end the story.

*Note about an error on page 40: The poem on page 40 entitled "The Bible," has a typo in the verse quoted at the head of the page (Psalm 138:2). The word typed "flame" is actually the word "Name." The text-recognition software used to create the book thought the N was a fl. Our apologies for this error!*

**REVERENCE FOR GOD'S WORD**

Understanding that, when we read the Bible, we are actually encountering the mind and thoughts of God Himself, and responding with appropriate honor.

**HUNGER FOR GOD'S WORD**

Being eager to learn what God has said to us, understanding that we are inadequate without it and need it as badly as we need food!

# THE HARVEST HOME

The second part of this book, *The Harvest Home*, is very different than the story of *The Bible in the Wall*, in at least four ways:

- First, it is not a story at all. It is an exhortation written in highly illustrative language.

- Second, it is written in much older English, so it may be a little harder to understand.

- Third, it is about England, not Italy and Switzerland as *The Bible in the Wall* was.

- Fourth, its theme is about thankfulness and how often we take God's gifts for granted and fail to tell Him "Thank you!" for His frequent favors.

We want to make the reader aware of these differences before starting this second portion of the book, and so you or your child don't think of it as a continuation of the previous story. We have only a few questions to suggest. Mostly, we just recommend a slow, careful reading of *The Harvest Home*, paying particular attention to the Psalms which are quoted.

1  Can you even imagine what it might be like to not have enough food to eat?

2  What does the sun and moon "taking up the language of praise" mean? (p. 45) The idea comes from Psalm 19.

3  Some key features to notice in this chapter are:

- The miracle of how food grows from the ground (page 47) and how this resembles resurrection, in the wisdom of God.

- The vast reach of the power of God, causing food to grow across the whole world (pages 48-49).

- Our unworthiness of God's provisions, as so often people do not serve Him and show no gratitude for all He has provided (pages 50-51).

4  How patient would you be with all the rebellion of sinners, if you were the God who had created us? Wow! What do you think?

How extremely dependent we are on God to provide for us (pages 52-53).

We ought to not only voice our thankfulness and gratitude to Him, but also, the obedience of our lives should show it (pages 54-55).

Consider finally that He has not only provided for the physical life of our bodies, but the blood of Christ and the Holy Spirit, that we might have eternal life (page 57).

1. Explain to your child how common this has been in many nations over the centuries, and how unusual it is that we in the U.S.A. have enjoyed such uninterrupted prosperity and sufficiency.

2. Your child may not be familiar with the idea of the sun and moon "taking up the language of praise." So, be sure to read Psalm 19 and see how that Psalm speaks of the sun and moon worshiping the Lord, merely by their very existence. They do what they were created to do! – they display the glory of God, in the immensity and glory of their created beauty. We get to glorify God with our words and actions. The sun and moon glorify God by their beauty and brilliance.

3. Discuss those key features.

4. As you talk about God's patience, look at these verses:

   • 2 Peter 3:9: God's patience will endure until every last one of the children He intends to save have been gathered.

   • Romans 2:4: God's patience has an aim: He means to give people time to repent.

   • 1 Timothy 1:16: Jesus Christ has already saved the very worst types of sinners, to demonstrate how patient He is. This should encourage any terrible sinner that there is still hope for him or her, too!

## Activities

1. Using an old book, try a game of hide and seek. Have one of the children hide it somewhere unusual and the others look for it later.

   OR even better: Find an old book in your home — one you don't care about the condition of, one you are willing to throw away. If you have an old barn or shed that you can put the book in, maybe into a hole in the wall there, try it. Don't wrap it with any protection. Then come back a long time later to see how it looks! Wait as long as you can, but go back to it one day.

2. In reference to *The Harvest Home* — try starting a list of all the things you can be thankful for. You'll be amazed soon how long the list becomes. You're liable to fill many pages of paper!

3. Try giving away Bibles in some public place, and as you do, count how many people are interested and how many people show no interest at all, even resistance. Then take some time afterwards to pray for those who received it (that they will read the Word and be converted), and to pray also for those who would not receive it (that they would start to hunger for the Word of God and desire it).

# GODLINESS IS GREAT GAIN
## Study Guide

This volume contains six stories on a variety of topics, and so we won't try to summarize here, except to say that they are about how God will bless honest work, honest service to others, and being thoughtful of those around us.

# Chapter One:
# THE WORK-HOUSE APPRENTICE

Though no specific year is mentioned in the story, its time is the mid-1800s in the town of Cornwall, in England.

1   What is an orphan?

2   Have you ever had someone you should obey tell you what to do, and then someone else you also should obey tell you to do the opposite? What did you do? How would you handle this? (page 1)

3   The Bible tells us to "Give thanks in all circumstances. For this is the will of God in Christ Jesus for you." (1 Thess. 5:18, ESV) Have you tried to be thankful in all circumstances? This is not easy to do!

Robert shows exceptional character, as we are told at the bottom of page 1: "Robert was not one to complain. He accepted his lot in life and was thankful that it wasn't worse." So, when you have a lot to be unhappy about and you could complain, what can you do in that hard situation to be able to give thanks?

4   How did Robert start to grow in Christian character when he began to learn the Word of God and follow the Lord?

5   Thinking about the memory verse, Ephesians 6:5: Why would the Apostle Paul tell slaves to be obedient rather than to fight back or escape?

## Memory Verses

### Proverbs 10:4

"A slack hand causes poverty, but the hand of the diligent makes rich." (ESV)

"He becometh poor that dealeth with a slack hand; but the hand of the diligent maketh rich." (KJV)

### Ephesians 6:5

"Slaves, obey your earthly masters with fear and trembling, with a sincere heart, as you would Christ." (ESV)

"Servants, be obedient to them that are your masters according to the flesh, with fear and trembling, in singleness of heart, as unto Christ." (KJV)

1   Robert, our hero in this first story, is an orphan. It would be good to explain the meaning of being an orphan to your child. You may even know one of those rare children, in our own country, who is in that tragic position of having lost both of his parents.

    In past centuries, such children often had it much worse than today. No one would feel any affection for them, and they usually did not have a chance to go to school and learn, but were forced into work and often treated very much like slaves. So Robert has to do the hardest chores. Try to help your child to feel how different a life this would be!

2   Help your child to understand responsible and sensible ways to handle this dilemma. One is, to notify each of those who are bossing you what the other said, and ask them to get together to decide what you should do. This makes it a decision that has to be worked out between them, not a conflict between you and either of them.

3   Your model, parent, will be crucial for this lesson to stick. Have your children heard you give thanks for your blessings, or for God's work in even painful and unwelcome events, accomplishing His purpose? If they have, you will know how to convey this. Show him that there is much more happening at any given time than the one thing which displeases us; there is usually much else that is still good which is ours.

4   Answers: enjoyment of worship, hunger and thirst for the Word of God (page 4), truthfulness, obedience, faithfulness to work diligently (page 5).

    And! – Robert's faithfulness resulted in promotion to a job with an actual salary! He began to earn money, being paid for his work (page 10).

5   Explain the Roman world of those times. Many were slaves due to being captive soldiers in a war; others were slaves because they had committed crimes and work was their penalty; still others were slaves because they had gotten into more debt than they could pay, so they had to work it off. So it wasn't always wrong for someone to be a slave. Sometimes the owners had a right to the labors of the slave.

    But even in cases in which it was completely wrong to own a slave, it would have been futile and probably deadly to try to fight back or escape. A slave might have gotten a beating for that, or in some cases, worse.

# Chapter Two:
## OUR FELLOW CLERK

1  Why did the employees think Mr. Westerton was selfish? Do they have any good reasons for that opinion of him? Do you agree or disagree?

2  What did the employees not know about Mr. Westerton which changed their opinion of him, once they discovered it? And what does that tell us about how we judge people?

3  What are the dangers and temptations of the theater, which the story speaks of? (page 17) And do we face any parallel or similar danger today?

4  The author (page 23) seems to have expected Mr. Westerton would explain his frugal habits as, saving up money to use for generous plans for others, but he did not. Why might someone who is very generous not tell others about it?

5  A key statement about this chapter is summed up in this Bible verse – 1 Samuel 16:7: "For the Lord sees not as man sees: man looks on the outward appearance, but the Lord looks on the heart." What is the difference between how the Lord sees people and how people see themselves and others?

6  How might we honor and love our parents when we are adults?

## Memory Verse

### 1 Samuel 16:7

"Man looks on the outward appearance, but the Lord looks on the heart." (ESV)

"For the Lord seeth not as man seeth: for man looketh on the outward appearance, but the Lord looketh on the heart." (KJV)

1   The grounds for thinking Mr. Westerton selfish and mean are very shallow. The men who judged his character in this way were not thinking sensibly nor were they considering that there are many other ways to explain and interpret his actions. We have to learn to judge with righteous judgment, as Jesus said (John 7:24).

2   What they were unaware of was, his generosity (page 17). Also, this tells us that when we judge other people, there's often a lot about others that we do not know which might change our opinion if we did.

3   Unguarded use of the television, or going to see movies without any discretion, can lead to a lot of sin. We need to always be careful about what we see; it can corrupt us by strengthening ungodly desires in our hearts.

4   Look at Matthew 6:1-4 and see that we are instructed to refrain from boasting about our generosity; that a godly man will not try to make sure others notice his generosity, to gain their respect. A godly man is content that the Lord knows and approves.

5   The Lord can see thoroughly and within; we can only see partially and from the outside. The Lord knows people's thoughts. We can only guess what they are thinking from their actions.

6   The duty to honor parents does not end when we are grown up and no longer children. We can still respect them and treat them as important to us.

# Chapter Three:
# THE TWO JOURNEYS

1  Have you ever been outside with someone who was not prepared for the cold? What did you do?

2  "Bull's Mouth" and "Hen & Chicks" (page 23) are very funny names for places, aren't they? England uses names like that. But we have towns in the U.S.A. with some very funny names, too.

   Can you find some towns or places in our country with such funny names?

3  When you choose to pay something for someone else as a gift to them, should you expect them to pay you back later?

4  Maybe you have wanted to be rich. Do you believe wanting to be rich leads to a lot of joy or a lot of pain?

5  Why should Arthur end his engagement? (pages 38-39)

6  Ecclesiastes 11:1 is quoted on page 41. This is an unusual Hebrew expression – throw bread in the water? What do you think it means?

## Memory Verse
### Ecclesiastes 11:1

"Cast your bread upon the waters, for you will find it after many days." (ESV)

"Cast thy bread upon the waters; for thou shalt find it after many days." (KJV)

1   Always try to think of a way to relieve their distress, even if it involves sharing what is yours with them. Remember, "Blessed are the merciful, for they shall receive mercy." (Matthew 5:7)

2   Examples: New Mexico has a town named "Truth or Consequences." There is also: Boring, Oregon; Lick Skillet, Tennessee; and lots of others!

3   See Luke 6:32-36 for an answer. We should be generous and expect the Lord to take care of us, expecting nothing in return from people. It may not sound safe or wise, but it is always safe to trust in the Lord rather than men.

4   The Bible says wanting to be rich will bring a person a lot of pain and misery! 1 Timothy 6:10

5   There was an expectation that, if he was going to marry and become a husband, that he would have a way to provide for his wife. This is often not thought about today; men do not prepare for being a provider for the family, as they ought to.

6   By "on the waters" it refers to shipping, which was how many goods were delivered long distances in those days (and often still are). Ship food – something you must have – to others when they need it. And when you need food, God will see to it that food is sent to you, too.

# Chapter Four:
## THE ONE TALENT

1   What does a "talent" mean in the story?

2   What is the smallest amount of food you have ever had in your house? Or, have you known any people who had very little food at home, or who even ran totally out?

3   Page 44 quotes the words from Scripture, "bread shall be given him; his waters shall be sure." This is a quote from the King James Version of Isaiah 33:16.

Do you remember what this means, from what we learned in Ecclesiastes in the previous chapter?

4   Have you ever read the Bible out loud to others? (page 45)

5   What does it mean to "hide your talent"? (page 47)

6   Page 53 gives us a hint what kind of talent even a poor person may have. Do you see it?

7   Do you know what your spiritual gifts are?

8   The story ends on page 54 with Mrs. Warner quoting to herself the words, "I am not my own; I am bought with a price." What does this mean?

## Memory Verse
### 1 Corinthians 6:19-20

"Or do you not know that your body is a temple of the Holy Spirit within you, whom you have from God? You are not your own; for you were bought with a price. So glorify God in your body." (ESV)

"What? Know ye not that your body is the temple of the Holy Ghost which is in you, which ye have of God, and ye are not your own? For ye are bought with a price: therefore glorify God in your body, and in your spirit, which are God's." (KJV)

1  Read "the parable of the talents" in Matthew 25:14-30. It is mentioned on page 45 and this will greatly increase your understanding of the story.

   A talent is not a skill or ability, as our word "talent" means; rather, it was a monetary unit, like a dollar.

2  Just a topic on which you should be able to have some interesting conversation that leads to thanksgiving!

3  It is again a reference to how God will "deliver" bread to us and take care of our needs.

4  It can be a really good idea and a great way to learn the Word of God together. Maybe you could plan to do this with a friend!

5  In Bible times, when a person was worried about losing his money, he might bury it in the ground somewhere. This was not very smart, as there have almost always been safe ways to invest your money and earn more with it, as a result.

   The meaning here when the story speaks of Mrs. Warner is, she was using her ability to serve the Lord with what she had. We should all do that, no matter how small it is.

   Is there any small way, in which you could serve the Lord, that you have buried and are not using, because it just seems too little to bother with?

6  The top of the page mentions kindness and generosity. Romans 12 and 1 Corinthians 12 tell us that some Christians have the spiritual gift of generosity, or service, mercy, or even "helps."

7  This is definitely a topic worthy of some conversation! Look through Ephesians 4, Romans 12 and 1 Corinthians 12 to see the lists of spiritual gifts.

   1 Peter 4:10-11 simplifies spiritual gifts into two categories: Some people have spiritual gifts of the teaching kind. Other people have spiritual gifts of the serving kind.

8  What she had in mind was the truth stated in 1 Corinthians 6:19-20.

# Chapter Five:
# GREAT EXPECTATIONS

1  Do you know what an inheritance is? The first sentence mentions a young man learning that he "was going to receive an inheritance."

2  There are people who feel that certain types of work are "beneath them"; they think they deserve to have a better job than that and only people less important than they should have to do that work.

Is there a certain kind of job you would feel humiliated to have to do? (garbage pickup man, for instance)

Show your child from Ephesians 6:5-9 that all work can be done "as to the Lord" and so, in any job, it is possible to honor God in how we serve.

3  Page 61 mentions the love of money being a root of all kinds of evil. If you were to love money too much, what evils would it lead to in your life?

4  Why did the news of his coming inheritance affect Aaron so that he no longer worked hard?

## Memory Verse

### 1 Timothy 6:10

"For the love of money is a root of all kinds of evil. It is through this craving that some have wandered away from the faith and pierced themselves with many pangs." (ESV)

"For the love of money is the root of all evil; which while some coveted after, they have erred from the faith, and pierced themselves through with many sorrows." (KJV)

1. An inheritance is when someone who has died, has their money and all things they own passed on to someone else – usually to their children, but sometimes to other people they are grateful for.

2. Show your child from Ephesians 6:5-9 that all work can be done "as to the Lord" and so, in any job, it is possible to honor God in the way we serve. If there is a way to love God while we do it, and show love to others by serving them, then we can do it to the glory of God!

3. Notice, some Bible translations give us the impression that the love of money is the root of ALL evil; but that is an overstatement. The Apostle Paul actually said in 1 Timothy 6:10 that the love of money is a root that leads to all types of evil.

4. He foolishly assumed that the money he had been given would last and last, and that it wasn't necessary for him to work anymore. Never think in such a foolish way! No matter how much you have been given, it's always safest to keep working somewhere and keep earning.

*Provide the Dictionary Definition*

DILIGENCE

_____

_____

_____

RESPONSIBILITY

_____

_____

_____

# Chapter Six:
## A LICHFIELD TALE

1 Why would Edward see being reproved by the Lord as a mark of being shown His love and mercy? (page 70)

2 Why did Anne's mother say to her "Rich enough is a rare state to find?" (page 71)

3 Anne asks herself on page 75 if she has practiced "self-denial." What do you think that means?

4 Do the rich always have more advantages than the poor? What does the story tell us about this?

## Memory Verse
### Proverbs 21:5

"The plans of the diligent lead surely to abundance, but everyone who is hasty comes only to poverty." (ESV)

"The thoughts of the diligent tend only to plenteousness; but of everyone that is hasty only to want." (KJV)

1  Hebrews 12:5-11 and Psalm 141:5 show that being reproved is a blessing from the Lord. For if we are always enjoying people's approval, we never get corrected and pretty soon we will never be growing or changing anymore.

2  Because no matter how much money people have, they usually want still more. It is rare for people to have the content state of mind (attitude).

3  Self-denial is a phrase rarely heard from people today, but it comes from Luke 9:23. Jesus taught that sometimes, obeying God will require we deny our own desires, and at times have to do things which would not normally be our choice to please ourselves, but to please others or to do the will of God. For, often our desires are fleshly and selfish desires.

4  Definitely not! The rich have one advantage over the poor, but there are a lot of other blessings which are just as important as having lots of money – some of them much more important! Riches can even be a curse which make a person very unhappy.

## Activities

1  Do you know anyone whom you have judged hastily and mistakenly? If so, ask the Lord to forgive you for that, and if you have treated them in that way, and feel you wronged them personally, confess it to them also.

2  Most of us have more clothing than we need. Can you take some clothing to a rescue mission, a women's shelter, or somewhere that needy people could use some more clothes? Perhaps you don't know anyone who hasn't got the clothes they need, but especially if it's winter and you live near a city, you can find some people living outside who need a coat or some sort of warmer clothing. Go visit them and take some! Note: Do this in groups and not alone or just with your Mom. Better to have at least one man along too, for some of these people are not always entirely safe.

# LITTLE DAISY AND
# THE SWEARING CLASS
## Study Guide

Daisy's trials have been heavy, painful, and many. But she has not forgotten what was taught her about controlling her tongue and the power of words to do good or harm. She certainly knows that there is some talk that deeply dishonors God. While doing her work as a seller of flowers on the street, Daisy meets many who are careless about what they say, and to her great surprise, she has a role in teaching even adults to be more conscientious about their speech and what God thinks of it.

# Chapter One:
# THE LITTLE FLOWER-GIRL

1  Do you know what an oath means? Page 6 mentions "a fearful oath burst from his lips."

2  Page 6 mentions that General Forster's language had gradually changed and now he was in a "bad habit" of speaking this way.

   Do you have any bad habit? Is it something you used to never do, that now you do frequently? How can that be changed?

3  Why do you think people will be ashamed of using curse words in front of people, but it does not bother them that the Lord hears? (page 7)

## Memory Verse

### James 1:26

"If anyone thinks he is religious and does not bridle his tongue but deceives his heart, this person's religion is worthless." (ESV)

"If any man among you seem to be religious, and bridleth not his tongue, but deceiveth his own heart, this man's religion is vain." (KJV)

1   *Oath* was an old word to describe someone who used what we would call a curse word today.

2   Speak to your child about the sanctifying power of the Holy Spirit which is available to those who seek Him for it. He sanctifies through the truth of the Word – John 17:17 – so first, we must know what the Word calls us to, and then we must request the Spirit to enable us to walk in it.

3   People have this tragic ability to ignore what God hears and sees, because He is not visible to us as men are.

*Activity*

Ask a friend if they see a
bad habit in you: mean words
that you say, or bad attitudes
you show (grumbling or bitterness).
Hear their opinion respectfully
and commit to pray about
what they had to say!

# Chapter Two:
# A CLUSTER OF DAISIES

1  Page 13 quotes Exodus 20:7, which is part of the third commandment, about taking the name of the Lord in vain. What exactly is it to break this command?

2  Page 14: What a remarkable discovery, to learn that "I have treated the Almighty with less reverence and respect than I show my fellow man." This was an amazingly clear way to put it. Have you ever done that?

3  Have you ever had to deliver words of correction to an adult? Was it hard? How did you go about it, and was it different than the way you would correct someone your own age?

## Memory Verse

### Isaiah 8:13

"But the Lord of hosts, Him you shall honor as holy. Let Him be your fear, and let Him be your dread." (ESV)

"Sanctify the Lord of hosts Himself; and let Him be your fear, and let Him be your dread." (KJV)

1  Taking the Lord's name in vain is not merely the only way this is done; the one thing people usually think of is, when they hear people use God's name in cursing (we leave it up to you, parent, to decide whether to show your child what you mean, by saying that phrase out loud to your children, or not. How you convey this point to them may depend on whether they have heard this before or not). The full truth is, people take the Lord's name in vain anytime they speak of God casually, lightly, as a joke, or not seriously.

2  This should lead to some very good discussion with your child. Anyone should be able to think of times when you respected other people's wishes more than you did those of the Lord.

3  See 1 Timothy 5:1-2 to realize that we are not to rebuke an older person, but appeal to or entreat them. That means, we speak gently and not harshly; asking and not bossing.

*Activity*

Parents: Are we open to
correction from our children?
Have we instructed them as to how
to respectfully entreat us?
Always know that how we speak
in the home is how our children
will learn from us to
speak to others.

# Chapter Three:
# THE DAISY TRANSPLANTED

1   Do you know what a "boarding school" is? (page 27)

2   If you heard someone else taking the name of God in vain, what would you say to correct them about it?

3   Jack clearly disliked hearing sinful speech around him and so did not associate with other boys who spoke that way. Have you had friends who were prone to speak in evil ways? You weren't necessarily wrong for keeping them as friends; you may have other reasons. But did your friendship with such a person have any bad affects on you?

## Memory Verse

### Exodus 20:7

"You shall not take the name of the Lord your God in vain, for the Lord will not hold him guiltless who takes His name in vain." (ESV)

"Thou shalt not take the name of the Lord thy God in vain; for the Lord will not hold him guiltless that taketh His name in vain." (KJV)

1. Boarding schools are a place where children to go live, away from their families, and do school there. Sometimes missionaries who do not want their children to live in a dangerous nation, where they live, will send their children to a boarding school.

2. The phrase comes from the 3rd commandment of the Ten, in Exodus 20:7: "You shall not take the name of the Lord your God in vain, for the Lord will not hold him guiltless who takes his name in vain."

3. Try delicately but firmly to help your child recall relationships with other children, and their conduct, which may have had a bad affect on him; and give thanks together if there have not been some of these!

*Activity*

Take time to pray that God would give you friendships with people who will build you up in the faith and encourage you by their godly conduct and conversation!

# Chapter Four:
## DAISY'S SISTER FLOWERETS

1  If your child is not familiar with the Egyptians pyramids and The Sphinx, look them up in a book or on the internet to show them.

2  What is "the Golden Rule" to which page 37 refers?

3  We may find it curious that the little girl who dropped the Bibles was regarded as having sinned when she said, "Oh! Bother the old things!" We probably would not say this at all; or if we did, we would not say it with those words. How would you re-phrase in today's language, what she was saying? Why was it wrong to say?

### Memory Verse

**Matthew 7:12**

"So whatever you wish that others would do to you, so do to them; for this is the Law and the Prophets." (ESV)

"Therefore all things whatsoever ye would that men should do to you, do ye even so to them; for this is the law and the prophets." (KJV)

## Answers for Chapter Four:

1   This should be easily done with whatever sources you can use.

2   Matthew 7:12: "So whatever you wish that others would do to you, do also to them, for this is the Law and the Prophets."

3   She was saying something equivalent to "Who cares about these old books? They don't mean anything to me!" One should never speak so carelessly and lightly about our Bible. I hope that each of you who are reading this would value your Bible far more than that, and even value your other good books more than this, but especially the Word of God.

# Chapter Five:
# DAISY: A STUDY

1  Do you know any child who has suffered a tragedy which has set back their ability to learn?

2  Why would words like "mercy, gracious, goodness, good heavens," bother Daisy? (page 46). Do you think that, at one time, Christian people worried too much about such things, or that Daisy was right to take offense?

3  If you have ever found yourself reluctant to correct someone for a bad habit (like Daisy was), why were you? What would help you to get past that and do what you should?

4  When should you not correct someone and instead leave them alone?

## Memory Verse
### Proverbs 10:20

"The tongue of the righteous is choice silver; the heart of the wicked is of little worth." (ESV)

"The tongue of the just is as choice silver; the heart of the wicked is little worth." (KJV)

1    Help your child to thoughtfully and tenderly comprehend the difficulties which this child suffers; perhaps you can think of ways to help whoever it is.

2    Our personal opinion (compilers of this study guide) is that, regarding these phrases as offensive to God or sinful is a stretch; we cannot see why they would be wrong. But we understand the desire to not use lightly words which speak of reverent topics and respect those who think otherwise.

3    We have to remember in those moments that it is our duty nonetheless to do it, even when it's hard; and that the Lord equips us with His help when we do what is right. Especially when it's difficult to do.

4    When we are not sure that we are judging their behavior by biblical standards. If their action is merely bothering us but is not sin (according to the Word's definitions of sin) then we should not consider it our business to be correcting them, but rather correct our own attitude about them.

## Activity

Write down something that bothers you when people do it or say it, even though you are not sure at all that it is a sin. How should you respond to those types of things when they happen?

# Chapter Six:
# DAISY: A TEACHER

1    Who would "Lady Queen Fair" be? (page 49)

2    In this chapter, is Daisy being righteous or being fussy over nothing, to criticize the children for saying "The Lord knows," or to concern herself with a Bible being used as a prop? Would you use a Bible as a doorstop, or as part of a toy fort you were building?

3    Daisy has what we call "a tender conscience," sometimes in the New Testament referred to as a "weak conscience." This is when someone believes they are sinning, even at times when they have done nothing wrong. Talk with your child about whether he or she has this problem at all.

## Memory Verse

### Romans 14:10

"Why do you pass judgment on your brother? Or you, why do you despise your brother? For we will all stand before the judgment seat of God." (ESV)

"But why dost thou judge thy brother? Or why dost thou set at nought thy brother? For we shall all stand before the judgment seat of Christ." (KJV)

1    This was a way of speaking of "playing Queen" – that is, a game of pretending to be the Queen of England.

2    It certainly would be better to not use the Bible as though it were a building block! It is the Word of God and should be treated with respect. It doesn't mean that we consider the cover and papers to be sacred or holy things; but they do contain God's Word, and that should be enough to make us treat them with honor.

3    Read Romans 14 to see that Christians used to feel this way over certain foods, and judge one another over it. This was not necessary. The two important factors are: Not to judge each other for what we cannot show from the Word of God is wrong, and yet also: not to try to persuade people to do things that they feel guilty about. If it bothers their conscience (even if the Bible allows it) they should not do it.

# Chapter Seven:
## THE SWEARING CLASS

1  Why would Daisy not swear on her sacred word and honor? (page 62)

2  How would you respond if Jesus were to come down and walk with us, as page 66 talks about? In what ways would it make you careful?

3  In what way is Jesus just as present with us as if He was here in person?

4  What do you think of the usage of words like "golly, gee, darn, heck"? Are they slang for greater realities, as page 68 suggests?

5  Whether you agree or disagree with some of the specifics, how important is it for us to guard our lips, as the verse on page 70 (Psalm 141:3) mentions? Look at James 1:26 also.

## Memory Verse

### Psalm 141:3

"Set a guard, O Lord, over my mouth; keep watch over the door of my lips." (ESV)

"Set a watch, O Lord, before my mouth; keep the door of my lips." (KJV)

1   This is what Jesus taught in Matthew 5:34-37 – to reinforce your promises by saying it "on" something, is a bad habit. It's a way of saying, you didn't really mean what you promised unless you enforced it with some additional words. For instance, you may have heard someone say "Scout's honor, I mean it!"

2   Of course we would all be more careful if the Lord Jesus was personally present and we could see that He was watching our actions with His own eyes. But we should know that His watching us right now is just as real as it would be if we could see Him with us.

3   He told us that, when He sent the Holy Spirit, that it was in effect like Him coming to us. John 14:18; and even that it was advantageous for Him to leave (physically) so that the Holy Spirit would come (John 16:7).

4   While many of us don't think of the words *God, Jesus, damn,* or *hell* (all of those are legitimate words that are used in the Bible) when we see *golly, gee, darn,* or *heck* — those are actually what they were originally substitutes for. So it might in fact be wiser not to casually use those terms.

5   If we do not guard our lips and be careful about what we speak, our religion is worthless, James says. We do not show one of the most basic fruits of the Spirit: self-control.

# Chapter 8:
# DAISY'S NAME

1 Instead of the usual chapter questions, let's just ask this for today: What does the Bible have to say about guarding our tongues? Do your own study of it. Find as many Scriptures on it as you can (no less than 5).

## Memory Verse

Pick from among the verses mentioned in the "answers" on the following page.

1  Among the verses that your child should find, some for instances are:

   • Psalm 15:3, Psalm 34:13, Psalm 120:2

   • Proverbs 10:31, Proverbs 12:18-19

   • James 3:1-10

*Definitions*

**SELF-CONTROL**

The ability do the right thing from the heart, without being compelled or controlled by outer events, other people, or our emotions.

**REVERENCE**

Treating someone or something with the deepest possible respect.

# Chapter Nine:
# THE LOST FOUND

1   Page 83 says the General and his wife "never gossiped." Do you know what gossip is?

2   What does it mean that "they came trooping in gently, and with soft footsteps, as became the house of God"? (page 86)

3   Have you ever had a reunion with someone you never expected to see again?

### Memory Verse

### Ecclesiastes 5:2

"Guard your steps when you go to the house of God. To draw near to listen is better than to offer the sacrifice of fools, for they do not know that they are doing evil." (ESV)

"Keep thy foot when thou goest to the house of God, and be more ready to hear, than to give the sacrifice of fools: for they consider not that they do evil." (KJV)

1   This is a word and idea which is often misunderstood. Some think gossip is saying things about others that aren't true. No! – that's different. That is lying, sometimes referred to as slander.

A good definition of gossip is: Gossip is sharing information about people, with others, that they have no right to know and you have no right to share. Even if it's true, it can still be gossip.

2   It was a way of saying, they came to worship in an honorable way, not hurrying in and out, without a serious thought; but that they came reverently and thinking about how important what they were doing was.

3   Talk about this and what made it so meaningful.

## Activities

1   Are there any things you say as a habit that you really ought not to say? It would be good to ask your parents and even your brothers and sisters, for their opinion, before you settle on the decision that you never do any such thing.

2   Certainly it would not be rude or wrong to point out to the friends that they are speaking abusively of others, or disrespectfully of the Lord, in some of their speech. If they wish to honor God in their lives, they will be glad you told them. Do you have any friends to whom it would be a kind gesture from you, to correct some of how they speak when they are sad, annoyed, or careless?

# THE LITTLE MEDICINE CARRIER
## Study Guide

George Wayland has his first job! He is delivering medicines to the people in and around his village. But do you think this is easy? Friends tempt him to lie about money, to waste time; and he also discovers new opportunities to do good to others and be a blessing to them. Most of all, he learns to be honest whether people are watching or not, because the eye of God is always upon us.

# Chapter One:
# A JOB FOR GEORGE

1  Why does the poem that opens the chapter call Christians "the lambs of Jesus"?

2  Have you seen people waste time when they should be working? Why is this really a form of robbery? (page 3)

3  So, George is thrilled to be working for $6 per week (page 4). Would you work at a job that paid you $6 for the whole week?

4  Why does the Sunday School teacher say that we have "naturally sinful minds"? (page 6)

5  Why is stealing little things sinful, just like stealing big things? (what the story calls "picking," page 8).

6  Did you know it is actually a mark of a godly person to be kind to animals? Where do we learn this to be true?

*When memorizing Colossians 3:22, go on to talk a little about verses 22-25 (the context). Notice what these verses say about eye-service (working only when being watched) or being man-pleasers or people-pleasers. This is exactly the kind of delivery boy Doctor Bertram did not want!*

*Also, take time to note that, when this letter of Colossians was written, most employees were actually slaves. So, if they were to obey their masters, we can certainly apply that directly to anyone we are working for, when we are doing it much more willingly than slaves!*

## Memory Verse
### Colossians 3:22

"Slaves, obey in everything those who are your earthly masters, not by way of eye-service, as people-pleasers, but with sincerity of heart, fearing the Lord." (ESV)

"Servants, obey in all things your masters according to the flesh; not with eyeservice, as men-pleasers, but in singleness of heart, fearing God." (KJV)

1   Isaiah 40:11 and John 21:15 speak of the Lord's people as lambs, as well as a few other places in Scripture. It's a beautiful picture of little, weak and vulnerable ones being protected and led by a shepherd.

2   For answering this, it might help to refer to page 6: "He may forget that his time is no longer his own property when he begins working for someone else." Explain to your child that when you go to work for someone, the exchange is for your time for their pay. Thus, for that period of time (9 a.m. to 5 p.m., or whatever it is) your time is now the purchased property of the boss for whom you work. So, using any of it for yourself is stealing from him.

3   Of course, to your child, $6 / week will not sound like very much money at all! So, if needed, explain to your child how money has changed and inflated over the years. $6 was worth a lot more in the 1800s than it is now. This can become an entertaining and fascinating conversation, depending on how creative you can get about it!

4   This is a clear, biblical truth, which you can show from Jeremiah 17:9, Ephesians 4:18, Romans 12:1-2, and Genesis 6:5. Even though Genesis 6:5 speaks of the state of men's minds at the time of Noah's flood, nothing about men has changed since then.

5   Because he who is faithful with a little is one who will be faithful with much, as Jesus taught (Luke 16:10).

6   Proverbs 12:10 says so: "Whoever is righteous has regard for the life of his beast; but the mercy of the wicked is cruel."

The second part of that verse may be difficult for a child to understand. The meaning is, wicked people are sometimes cruel even when they think and feel like they are doing something merciful and kind. They just have terribly bad judgment about this!

# Chapter Two:
# GEORGE'S TEMPTATION

1 Think about how Satan tempts you! Too few people take time to consider this. We can see the ways he was trying to get to little George Wayland. How does he get to you?

2 Then – because it's so much more encouraging! – think also about: What are some ways the Holy Spirit helps you and equips you to resist temptation?

3 We are so prosperous in our nation today that, nearly no one who left out a bowl of oranges in their home would care if someone passing through picked one up. We would not consider it stealing for a person in the house to take one – even if they did not ask. Especially if we heard it was to give to his sick sister! But in older times, people did not have as much money. In light of that, is there anything we can still learn from this about wisdom in such decisions?

## Memory Verse

### 1 John 4:4

"Little children, you are from God and have overcome them; for He who is in you is greater than he who is in the world." (ESV)

"Ye are of God, little children, and have overcome them; because greater is He that is in you, than He that is in the world." (KJV)

1   Without tearing down or humiliating your child, gently help them to recognize some of the ways that temptation tends to effectively reach them, influence them, and even sometimes overtake and defeat them.

2   In talking about this, it will be wise to include people and surroundings the Lord has put in your child's life which have a role in providing protection from temptation: family, godly parents who read you good books, your church, power supplied by the Lord when we pray to ask for it (Matthew 6:13, Matthew 26:41), and most of all – the Lord Himself – 2 Peter 2:9 (the first phrase speaks of how the Lord knows how to rescue or deliver His people from temptation; some Bible versions use the word "trial," but it's the same word as is used elsewhere for temptation).

3   It is always wiser and safer to ask first, even if you think it will be OK. That way, you will be thought of as very polite, and will not be accused of doing wrong.

# Chapter Three:
## ENVY IN HIS HEART

1   How does envy in our hearts harm us? How does it dishonor God?

2   The words mentioned in the middle of page 32, "A soft answer turns away wrath, but a harsh word stir up anger," are from Proverbs 15:1.

  Do you have a friendship or relationship with anyone, in which you can apply this?

3   Why would James describe the human tongue as something that can be like a poison?

4   As the chapter ends, we see George realizing he does not have as much reason to envy Miss Beatrice as he thought. What does this tell us about the ways we envy others?

## Memory Verses

### Proverbs 15:1

"A soft answer turns away wrath; but a harsh word stirs up anger." (ESV)

"A soft answer turneth away wrath; but grievous words stir up anger." (KJV)

### Psalm 37:1

"Fret not yourself over evildoers; be not envious of wrongdoers." (ESV)

"Fret not thyself because of evildoers, neither be thou envious against the workers of iniquity." (KJV)

1 We are commanded not to envy others (1 Peter 2:1, Galatians 5:21).

It disrupts our peace and makes us agitated, upset, and discontent (Proverbs 14:30).

And – note this! – it is one of the sins that led to people crucifying the Lord Jesus! (Mark 15:10). So no good comes from envying others!

People can be envious of the money or things that other people have – their toys, their car, or even of their relationships (their husband or wife), or even of their job ("my job is horrible but his job is easy" – when the person saying things like that usually doesn't really know what trials or troubles there are at that other person's job).

2 It's likely your child knows someone with whom he can apply this as he relates to that person; either another child or even an adult, a relative perhaps.

3 This comes from James 3:8: "No human being can tame the tongue; it is a restless evil, full of deadly poison."

4 We need to see that their lives may not be as ideal or problem-free as we think.

## Definition

### ENVY

Being discontent or resentful of someone else's possessions, quality or "luck" and wishing we could have what they have.

# Chapter Four:
## MISS BEATRICE

1  Yesterday, George was envying Miss Beatrice. Today, he finds out that she envies him! What gift does George have from the Lord that she does not have?

2  Nelly (page 48) thought it was "lucky" for George to be there at the right time. But is "lucky" really the right way to describe this, or should we call it something else?

3  On page 41, the author writes of watching how boys and girls behave as they relate to adults, whenever he passes through a village. Do you notice this? What are some types of behavior you see from children that bother you?

## Memory Verse
### Proverbs 16:33

"The lot is cast into the lap, but its every decision is from the Lord." (ESV)

"The lot is cast into the lap, but the whole disposing thereof is of the Lord." (KJV)

1   George has the ability to run! Wouldn't you be sad if you were unable to do that?

2   As the next page explains, it was not luck at all: it was because George was responsible and was doing his job, and God blessed him and others in that path.

Note: when we try to explain any events with the word "lucky," we are really talking superstitious talk, which is nonsense. Saying "lucky" is actually offering no explanation for what happened at all.

3   Your child may name some behaviors observed in other children that perturb him, but if not, you can provide clues, bringing up things like interrupting, backtalking, or not being helpful, or more serious ones such as lying.

# Chapter Five:
# THE GIFT

1  Why did George write that the gift for his mother was "from the children" instead of from himself and Nelly only? What does this teach us? (page 52)

2  Page 54 quotes the saying of Jesus, "It is more blessed to give than to receive." I think we know that not everyone believes this. Why do they not believe it?

3  Whether people believe it or not, why is it true?

## Memory Verse
### Proverbs 11:25

"Whoever brings blessing will be enriched, and one who waters will himself be watered." (ESV)

"The liberal soul shall be made fat; and he that watereth shall be watered also himself." (KJV)

1   Since Willy did not have a gift for mother, George wanted to give him a chance to feel included. This shows that a great way to be thoughtful of others is to include them in a group effort and give them more credit than they are due.

2   Most of the reason people do not believe this is because they are selfish; they would really rather have things given to them than give to others. Sadly, they miss a blessing in life that they do not even seem to understand.

3   For one, being generous to others makes us more like God than being takers. Also, being generous to others provides us a unique type of pleasure and satisfaction, which is greater than just having a gift ourselves. It is the joy of seeing someone else made happy.

*Activity*

Think of an idea you can give as a gift to someone that comes from your whole family. You'll enjoy the blessing all together of making someone else very happy!

# Chapter Six:
# MACO'S NEW HOME

1  Why would anyone be happy that they are nearing death?

2  How would you feel if you knew you only had a few weeks to live?

3  Page 58 quotes 1 John 2:2, about Jesus being the propitiation for the sins of the world. Find a definition for the word "propitiation."

4  Have you ever been with someone who was dying? How did you feel about it, or how do you think you should feel, if you knew that person was a Christian?

## Memory Verses

### Philippians 1:21

"For me to live is Christ, and to die is gain." (ESV)

"For me to live is Christ, and to die is gain." (KJV)

### Revelation 21:4

"He will wipe away every tear from their eyes, and death shall be no more; neither shall there be mourning, nor crying, nor pain anymore; for the former things have passed away." (ESV)

"And God shall wipe away all tears from their eyes; and there shall be no more death, neither sorrow, nor crying, neither shall there be any more pain. For the former things are passed away." (KJV)

1. Page 57 tells us Miss Beatrice's response to drawing near the time of her death. She was not afraid of it, but rather looked forward to going to be with the Lord and the end of her sufferings. A lot of people feel this way – but it's only possible if you know for sure that you have trusted in the Lord Jesus Christ!

2. Discuss with your child, being sure to listen and not talk over them. Listen carefully for correct or incorrect ways of thinking about dying, and ask the Lord for wisdom to lead them carefully into biblical thinking.

3. Finding a way to appease or satisfy the wrath or anger of God.

4. While it is of course appropriate to feel that you would miss them, you should also be happy that they have gone to be with the Lord. After all, the Apostle Paul tells us that, for a Christian, "to die is gain." (Philippians 1:21)

## Activities

1. Who is the youngest friend of yours, who has a job outside of their home? That is, working for other people. Plan a time to visit with them and ask them, what kinds of challenges did they find happening to being honest or walking with God on that job?

2. Do you know anyone who is dying? You might be reluctant to visit them, because you are a little scared. Maybe it's uncomfortable and you don't know what to say. Or you are afraid they might die while you are there! But think about them instead of yourself and make that visit. Talk to them about pleasant things that you know they would enjoy.

# A LITTLE REBEL
# BECOMES A SAINT
## Study Guide

This story is meant to show a child that obedience must be learned in the path of various challenges in life. For all of us, this is a recurring lesson, that is, one which we have to learn again and again. Charles is especially difficult to teach and slow to learn, but perhaps being an orphan has tempted him to be stubborn and heartless towards others. It is no excuse, but we know that is a hard start to a child's life. Can Charles be taught to be kind? By the grace of God in Christ, he can.

# Chapter One:
## CHARLES AND HIS PUPPY

1 What is diphtheria?

2 The first pages of the book speak of God definitely hearing their prayers. How can we know God if hears our prayers?

3 What does the reference to "God's Book of Remembrance" mean? Have your child look this up in Scripture and write his conclusions.

4 Since Charles had been told to stay in the fenced yard, what should he have done when his puppy Bobby strayed outside the fence?

5 Page 8 speaks of how "disobedience is what made God send Adam and Eve out of that beautiful Garden of Eden." Why did God punish Adam and Eve in this serious way?

6 Who was that "wisest king that ever lived" mentioned near the end of the chapter on page 8?

## Memory Verse

### James 1:5

"If any of you lacks wisdom, let him ask God, who gives generously to all without reproach, and it will be given him." (ESV)

"If any of you lack wisdom, let him ask of God, that giveth to all men liberally, and upbraideth not, and it shall be given him." (KJV)

1  Diphtheria is a severe infection which can result in a sore throat, with intense swelling of the airway, often making it difficult to breathe. It can create a serious, lasting cough and inflame the skin and eyes, and even cause kidney problems and internal bleeding.

2  God does not send us some sort of "signal" that proves He has heard our prayers; that is, we can't see it in some physical way. Sometimes we can know by answers that He grants us. But more often, we can be assured that God hears our prayers by being careful to pray according to God's will. For, as 1 John 5:14 says, "And this is the confidence that we have toward Him, that if we ask anything according to His will, He hears us."

3  It is a reference to Malachi 3:16. The phrase probably means that God took careful note of those who feared Him (that is, who respected and honored Him more than anything or anyone else). It would be similar to the idea contained in the Book of Revelation when it says that there are names written in the Lamb's book of life.

4  Charles should have gone immediately to one of the adults and asked them to go retrieve the wandering puppy for him, rather than disobey and go out after Bobby himself.

5  Show your child the story of Adam and Eve in Genesis 3 and make sure he understands the huge consequences which came on the human race from this one act of disobedience. See Romans 5 and 1 Corinthians 15. As for themselves, they deserved the punishment of being banished from the garden because God had been so good to them; He had given them access to everything except for one tree, as a test – and they rebelled anyway. They no longer deserved the privilege of His presence.

6  That king was Solomon. 1 Kings 3:12 says that God gave Solomon wisdom unlike any other king before or after him, in answer to his prayer. This is encouraging to all of us, because James 1:5 says that God answers all prayers for wisdom positively and gives it. So use this to urge your child to always be seeking God for wisdom – which is, by the way, asking God for the power and skill to know how to do what is right.

*Definition*

## WISDOM

Wisdom is having the power and skill to carry out the obedience which you know is right.

# Chapter Two:
## CHARLES GOES TO SCHOOL

1   What is a spelling primer?

2   Find somewhere in the Bible that failing in life is compared to a shipwreck. What is this picture intended to mean?

3   Miss Owens advises Charles about the Bible, "Take it with you wherever you go." Other than carrying a Bible around with us everywhere (which is perhaps not what she meant), how can we practice this?

## Memory Verse

**Psalm 119:11**

"I have stored up Your word in my heart, that I might not sin against You." (ESV)

"Thy word have I hid in mine heart, that I might not sin against Thee." (KJV)

1   A "primer" is a first book of spelling and reading, for the child just starting out to learn how to read.

2   1 Timothy 1:18-19: "...wage the good warfare, holding faith and a good conscience. By rejecting this, some have made shipwreck of their faith."

    To say that someone shipwrecks means that their life has been destroyed, their moral compass is gone, and they could stray into any horrible behavior and sin.

3   Miss Owens might have meant that Charles should always keep a Bible with him, but more likely she meant that he should know it well and keep its truths constantly in his heart and mind. Of course, that will mean having a Bible around in your life all the time (not necessarily always on your person every minute) and will mean that you store up its commandments in your heart.

## Activity

Encourage your children to try to put the memory verse to a tune. Some can do it very easily and it makes it so much easier to memorize!

# Chapter Three:
# DROWNING THE SQUIRREL

1. Page 15 describes how Charles was horrified at first by the actions of boys at school, but after some time, their evil ways didn't bother him as much anymore. Why does this happen?

2. Why is cruelty to animals wrong? How is hunting different than what Charles was doing?

3. Find some Scriptures which show us that spending time with ungodly friends will affect you in bad ways, too, and tempt you to be ungodly.

4. Page 18 refers to "the ploughshare of affliction" as playing a part in preparing Charles's heart to walk with God. What does it mean by calling affliction a "ploughshare"?

## Memory Verse
### Psalm 119:67

"Before I was afflicted I went astray; but now I keep Your word." (ESV)

"Before I was afflicted I went astray; but now have I kept Thy word." (KJV)

1  Viewing and being around evil has a horrible affect on the conscience. The more of it we are exposed to and get used to, what begins to happen is, our heart hardens and we become less sensitive to how wicked it is. Sometimes the Bible calls this "a seared conscience" (2 Timothy 4:2), which means our conscience becomes deadened, the way a person's skin is deadened when it is burned.

2  Those who hunt animals for food are doing something God allows; and when a hunter shoots an animal, this nearly always results in a quick death which is not cruel nor intended to be cruel. But just torturing animals pointlessly is cruel because it causes a living thing suffering for no good reason. It is even worse when a person enjoys and thinks it is fun to cause a creature pain and misery, as Charles did!

3  1 Corinthians 15:33: "Do not be deceived: bad company ruins good morals."

Proverbs 22:24-25: "Make no friendship with a man given to anger, nor go with a wrathful man, lest you learn his ways and entangle yourself in a snare."

4  A ploughshare is the cutting edge or blade of a plow which makes the deep cut in the earth for a farmer when he is plowing. Affliction is sometimes compared to this, because it plows up our hearts and shows what is within us.

# Chapter Four:
## THE FORBIDDEN SWIM

1. Page 24 mentions Proverbs 13:1: "A wise son hears his father's instruction, but a scoffer does not listen to rebuke."

   None of us are excited about being rebuked. But we must learn to listen and welcome it, when appropriate. Can you think of times that you have not listened to rebuke?

2. Has there been an occasion when things would have turned out a lot better for you, if you had paid attention to someone's rebuke rather than react with annoyance to it?

3. Can you think of some biblical examples of someone being rebuked? Look up the ones you can think of in your Bible.

## Memory Verse
### Proverbs 15:32

"Whoever ignores instruction despises himself; but he who listens to reproof gains intelligence." (ESV)

"He that refuseth instruction despiseth his own soul; but he that heareth reproof getteth understanding." (KJV)

1  The one question in this chapter is certainly worth carefully exploring with your child. Don't let it all focus on your child, however. It could be helpful to him or her if you would share some of your own failures in this way.

2  Talk this through with your child, without embarrassing him about failure to listen to rebuke in the past. We've all done it!

3  A few examples in the Word that you might find are:

• Nathan rebuking King David for being unfaithful, 2 Samuel 12:7-12

• Paul rebuking Peter for being hypocritical, Galatians 2:11-14

• Jesus rebuking James and John for their harsh attitude, Luke 9:54-55

• God rebuking Job for being a know-it-all, Job 38:1-4

• Peter rebuking Ananias & Sapphira, Acts 5:1-5

## Definition

### REBUKE

When someone verbally corrects you
for your attitudes or actions, in hopes
of helping you to see it and change.

## Chapter Five:
## CHARLES AND HIS PARTRIDGE TRAP

1  Why would it be succumbing to temptation and sin to turn away from worship to go play games on Sunday? What does this say about those who prefer sports to Sunday worship?

2  What is the point of Ecclesiastes 10:20, as mentioned on page 29?

3  Why did Charles's lie make it difficult for him to pray? (page 31)

4  Notice that his mother told Charles that, if he was to stay home (even being sick!) he had to memorize Psalm 116. That is 19 verses long! What is the longest section of Bible you have ever memorized? Would you want to consider trying to memorize a whole chapter?

5  Page 34: Notice how wisely Charles's mother shows him his sin, by using the Ten Commandments. How many of the Ten Commandments can you list without looking at Exodus chapter 20?

6  What are some of the ways this chapter teaches that children may honor their parents, as it concludes?

## Memory Verse

### Psalm 66:18

"If I had cherished iniquity in my heart, the Lord would not have listened." (ESV)

"If I regard iniquity in my heart, the Lord will not hear me." (KJV)

1   It is so common today for even Christian families to let sports hinder them from worship, that most don't even see anything wrong with it anymore. But how can there be any question about this? Of course, allowing a game to interfere with God's command to not neglect worship with the church is very wrong. Hebrews 10:24-25 is clear enough on this point.

2   It means that God has amazing ways of getting the truth about the wrong things we have done to our parents or others whom we ought to have obeyed. Obviously, it is not birds who tell on us, but the news can travel fast, as if birds had delivered it in flight.

3   We see that it bothered his conscience. We know that we have lost the right to be asking God to do things for us when we are disobeying Him.

4   Maybe your child will not want to memorize an entire chapter, but see if he can be persuaded to aspire to aim at least for a little more than he has done in the past.

5   So often, we can find in the Law of God, a way to see our duty and our sin more clearly. Go over the Ten Commandments with your child and talk about what each means.

6   By obeying cheerfully (that means, without resentment or being annoyed, but happily); obeying quickly (without delays); from the heart; and respecting the fact that parents have wisdom from experience that children do not have.

# Chapter Six:
## THE SECOND LIE

1   Page 41: This is the third time Charles has used this terrible rationalizing to talk himself into following through with wicked plans to disobey and lie! What is wrong with this reasoning Charles uses in his heart? – that if he makes a promise to someone to sin, then he'd be lying to him to not follow through with it.

2   Why does the sin of lying grow so swiftly into a habit?

3   Charles's mother shows him that it's possible to be a liar in more than one way (page 42: by partly telling the truth and holding back part of the truth). Can you think of two or three other ways in which we can be sinfully deceptive, even if it is not an outright lie?

## Memory Verse

### Ephesians 4:25

"Therefore, having put away falsehood, let each one of you speak the truth with his neighbor, for we are members one of another." (ESV)

"Wherefore putting away lying, speak every man truth with his neighbor; for we are members one of another." (KJV)

1    Explain what ought to be done: If I have made plans to do evil with others and then it dawns on me that I must not, what should I do? Repent of the plans and tell the others that I've repented! It is never wrong to retract plans to do evil. It is always evil fully developed to follow through on those plans.

2    It becomes a habit for at least three reasons we thought of, and you may think of more! 1st, liars start to enjoy the power it gives them over people to deceive them.

Second, liars start to believe it makes life easier to make things up than to explain things according to truth.

Third, to avoid being caught, liars often are forced by their own lies to make up more lies to cover the previous ones.

3    Other ways people lie are, concealing evidence of the wrongs we have done or even that others have done; pretending to be better than we are. And you try to think of more.

---

## Definition

### HONESTY

---

Being someone who can be counted
on to speak and act truthfully
in all situations.

---

# Chapter Seven:
## MR. RAYMOND DIES

1  What is wrong with "cursing and swearing," as Charles's father, Mr. Raymond, had so commonly done?

2  Have you ever seen anyone die? How did it make you feel?

3  How could we say that God blesses some persons by withholding riches from them? (page 46)

4  Page 48: Charles would ask God to speak to him, and tell him if he was saved or lost. Is this how we find out if we are saved? If that is not the way, where can we find out?

## Memory Verse
### 1 Timothy 6:9-10

"But those who desire to be rich fall into temptation, into a snare, into many senseless and harmful desires that plunge people into ruin and destruction. For the love of money is a root of all kinds of evils. It is through this craving that some have wandered away from the faith and pierced themselves with many pangs." (ESV)

"But they that will be rich fall into temptation and a snare, and into many foolish and hurtful lusts, which drown men in destruction and perdition. For the love of money is the root of all evil: which while some coveted after, they have erred from the faith, and pierced themselves through with many sorrows." (KJV)

1   Some words in our language are considered abusive of others or descriptive of things in rude and harsh ways. There is no need to hurt or offend people by saying them.

2   If this has happened, feel free to talk it through with your child, but there is no need to dwell on it and make him uncomfortable with the memories. If it has never happened, find a gentle way to talk about how others have seen people die, and that it is painful to watch. Also talk about how something much more important is happening than someone's body dying; their existence is ending in this world and they are going to face God in the spiritual world.

3   God knows that, for some people, having riches would ruin them; it would only make them enslaved to various desires and pleasures, which they could easily buy anytime they wanted. It is not good for anyone to always be able to get whatever they want!

4   God's way is not to speak out loud to each of us about this. Rather, we can know and understand His thoughts about us by knowing His Word. He tells us what a godly person is like and what a wicked person is like in the Bible. We might think it would be great if God would speak out loud to each of us and tell us where we stand; but His method is rather, to tell us through His Word, the Bible, what a person who knows Him is like.

# Chapter Eight:
# CHARLES BECOMES PROFANE

1   What is it to ignore your conscience? (page 52)

2   Does the Bible say that gambling is a sin? Maybe not. But even if the Bible does not name gambling as a sin, is there anything about gambling which would demonstrate that it is, at least, very unwise or questionable?

3   As you think about Charles's life, consider that it is possible for an unsaved person to know so much of the Word of God that, it is impossible for him to enjoy either the world or the Lord. What is such a person to do to find relief of conscience and joy in life?

## Memory Verse

### Acts 24:16

"I always take pains to have a clear conscience towards both God and men." (ESV)

"Herein do I exercise myself, to have always a conscience void to offence toward God, and toward men." (KJV)

1   That is when we refuse to listen to that agitated or distressed feeling in our hearts that tells us we are doing the wrong thing.

2   The Bible does not name gambling as a sin, though it is possible that this is only because in most of the cultures in which the Bible was written, such an idea would not have been popular. Either way, it is foolish to risk the loss of money as a game. Money is too important to be played with as if it was a toy.

3   He should stop trying to please both the Lord and people, and realize that only pleasing the Lord is going to be rewarding in the long run. You cannot serve God and money, Jesus said (Matthew 6:24).

# Chapter Nine:
# FALSE RELIGION

1   The chapter begins by speaking of how the Holy Spirit was working in Charles, specifically in his conscience. How does the Holy Spirit do that?

2   Why do we know that Universalism is not true?

3   How is it that, time spent reading a book by an evil author is like spending time with that person? (page 60)

4   There is an ongoing battle within all of us between the sins that give us pleasure and the gospel truth we know. Talk about, what is that battle like for you? Not just for your child – talk about what it's like for you, too!

## Memory Verse

### Romans 6:16

"Do you not know that if you present yourselves to anyone as obedient slaves, you are slaves of the one whom you obey, either of sin, which leads to death, or of obedience, which leads to righteousness?" (ESV)

"Know ye not, that to whom ye yield yourselves servants to obey, his servants ye are to whom ye obey; whether of sin unto death, or of obedience unto righteousness?" (KJV)

1   He makes us remember things from the Bible we've been taught; He brings them back to mind. He also causes us to remember things godly people have taught us or said to us.

2   Jesus told us that many people are on the path to destruction and only a few are on the path to life. It warns us that hell will be the forever destiny of some people and heaven the eternal destiny of others.

3   Because we are exposed to his ideas and thoughts.

4   As you discuss this with your child, the goal is to make sure he or she knows that you struggle with sin just like he does. You cannot be a person who helps your child in the fight with sin if you are a hypocrite about having your own battle with sin.

# Chapter Ten:
## CHARLES PROPOSES

1  Where is Ohio? Can you find it on a map? Looking at the United States now, why was Ohio called "the far West" in this story? (page 63)

2  When pages 68-69 speak of (and underlines "and doeth them") the sayings Jesus calls upon us to do, what is the main / chief thing He calls on us to do? Does this mean we are only saved if we are obedient to all the things Jesus commands?

3  How will having a good wife, from the Lord, help keep a man walking in God's righteous paths? (Proverbs 19:14)

## *Memory Verse*
### Proverbs 19:14

"House and wealth are inherited from fathers, but a prudent wife is from the Lord." (ESV)

"House and riches are the inheritance of fathers: and a prudent wife is from the Lord." (KJV)

1    If geography is a topic of interest to your child (some children love maps!), explain why Ohio was considered "the far West" in those days. The reason is, the original colonies were almost all on the Atlantic seacoast, and just reaching the border of Ohio was over 400 miles further west! Perhaps you can find some maps online of Westward expansion which will help explain this.

2    The key thing Jesus wants us to do is believe in Him, trusting in His cross and His merits, and not our own works and righteousness (John 6:29).

3    Genesis 2:18 and Ecclesiastes 4:9-12 will help with answering this. Explain to your child how God has made men and women to be complementary to one another, by their unique differences not to clash but to assist each other in walking with God. Parents, tell your children about some of the ways in which your relationship as husband and wife has deepened your walk with God.

Genesis 2:18: "Then the Lord God said, 'It is not good that the man should be alone; I will make him a helper fit for him.'"

Ecclesiastes 4:9-12: "Two are better than one, because they have a good reward for their toil. For if they fall, one will lift up his fellow. But woe to him who is alone when he falls and has not another to lift him up! Again, if two lie together, they keep warm, but how can one keep warm alone? And though a man might prevail against one who is alone, two will withstand him - a threefold cord is not quickly broken."

# Chapter Eleven:
## STRUGGLING FOR FAMILY WORSHIP

1   Why do Charles's sins bother him so much all the time?

2   What is "family worship"?

3   Even when we feel as if we don't know how to pray or what to say, should we anyway? Why or why not?

## Memory Verse
### Psalm 34:11

"Come, O children, listen to me; I will teach you the fear of the Lord." (ESV)

"Come, ye children, hearken unto me; I will teach you the fear of the Lord." (KJV)

1  He is experiencing guilt about sin because of the faithful work of the Holy Spirit in his conscience. The Holy Spirit is at work convincing people of our sin, our need for righteousness, and the fact that judgment is coming (John 16:8). Also, in Charles's case, it's because he is so double-minded. He keeps living uncertain whether he wants to walk with God or be "of the world." Show your child what an agonizing way of life this is; few people are more miserable than those who can't make up their minds, whether they want to walk with God or continue in sin. Follow the Lord decisively!

2  Family worship is a phrase used by people to describe a time when the head of a household – usually the Dad – gathers all the members of the family to read the Bible and pray together. This used to be the habit of many American homes, became a rare occurrence during the 20th century, but we are seeing a little revival of it again in some Christian homes. It can be one of the most wonderful and profitable things for a family to do together! It need not be long – just five or ten minutes of reading and prayer can be a great benefit.

3  There are lots of good reasons to pray, even when we don't know what to say.

For one, it pleases God more that we try to pray, than to not call on Him at all.

Also, sometimes when we are so unsure of what words to say that we only moan and groan in God's presence, Romans 8:26-27 says that those are often times when the Holy Spirit is helping us to pray!

Last of all, if we don't know how to pray very well, we certainly won't learn by not trying. Most people who pray will tell you they learned more about prayer just by doing it – praying – than anything else.

*Activity*

How about you try to write a
Prayer List? Include missionaries
you know, your church leaders, the
President and others in government,
unsaved people you know, church
friends and family members.

# Chapter Twelve:
# PASTOR JOHNSON'S VISIT

1   How do the atonement and intercession of Jesus the Son of God comfort us? (page 81)

2   Why does Genesis 6:3 say man's days (lifespan) shall be 120 years? Most of us don't know anyone who has ever lived 120 years!

3   Have you experienced any of this work of the Spirit in your heart that Pastor Johnson describes to Charles? Which of these has been your experience?

## Memory Verse

### John 3:21

"But whoever does what is true comes to the light, so that it may be clearly seen that his works have been carried out in God." (ESV)

"But he that doeth truth cometh to the light, that his deeds may be made manifest, that they are wrought in God." (KJV)

1   Most of us know how the *atonement* of Jesus comforts us: being aware that He died for our sins is very comforting and encouraging! Our guilt before God is taken away, because He took it on for us!

But very few people think these days about comfort from the *intercession* of Jesus. It's a truth we read of in Hebrews 7:25, Isaiah 53:12, and Romans 8:34 (look up each of these verses). Do you know that, even after He sacrificed Himself on our behalf, He prays – so that this is not just a thing of the past, done a long time ago. Jesus lives in heaven and is constantly in prayer reminding His Father of what He did for us, and praying for us to have all the blessings and benefits that His death for us entitles us to. We, His people, are never off His mind, and are constantly in His prayers!

2   To rightly interpret the Bible, we have to know what the statement meant at the time it was given, to the people it was said to then. And what we know from reading the book of Genesis is, previous to this, many people lived for hundreds of years, some living almost 1,000 years! But after the flood, it appears that, as a form of judgment, God would cause most people to live around 120 years. But even if that was His plan then, it has not been His plan always nor was it promised to be. It may be that the shorter lifespan people commonly have now (more like 70 or 80 years) is a continuing mark of God's judgment on the human race for our sinfulness.

3   Listen to your child talk about how his sins make him feel, whether he goes through guilty feelings about them or pretty much ignores them. This would be a good time to also talk about what thoughts go through his mind when hearing sermons in church or when he hears conversations among people about walking with God.

# Chapter 13:
## CHARLES GOES TO CHURCH

1. Why do Christians sometimes feel unworthy to take the Lord's Supper? (what page 91 calls "the Lord's table")

2. Have you ever gone to church expecting God to do some striking thing that you would deeply feel, as Charles did in this chapter? Did it happen or not? Was your expectation of this helpful to you spiritually or not so much?

3. Charles sure has a lot of "ups" and "downs" when it comes to his walk with God. Do you think this is normal or is he an odd guy?

## Memory Verse
### Proverbs 24:16

"For the righteous falls seven times and rises again, but the wicked stumble in times of calamity." (ESV)

"For a just man falleth seven times, and riseth up again: but the wicked shall fall into mischief." (KJV)

1 Sometimes people think about their sins so much, they don't feel that they deserve to partake of this symbol of Jesus' death. They fear that their sinfulness shows that they are taking Him lightly. We must all evaluate ourselves sincerely about this.

2 While it is good to show up at church with a sense of anticipation that God will speak to us through His Word, it's not wise to be living in expectation of something earth-shaking every time. God's Word grows us as food does, with a gradual and cumulative effect.

3 It is not the same with everyone, but for most believers, their Christian life does consist of lots of ups and downs. See Proverbs 24:16.

# Chapter Fourteen:
# CHARLES AND THE SUNDAY SCHOOL

1  Page 98: Why would anyone be opposed to a Sunday School?

2  What is revival? Define what it is as well as some things it is not (for instance, it's not just having special meetings at your church).

3  Why does the writer compare Charles's decisions with the Israelites at the Red Sea, on page 103? What's the similarity?

## Memory Verse

### 2 Timothy 2:2

"And what you have heard from me in the presence of many witnesses, entrust to faithful men who will be able to teach others also." (ESV)

"And the things that thou hast heard of me among many witnesses, the same commit thou to faithful men, who shall be able to teach others also." (KJV)

1    It's because of the history of Sunday Schools. Churches used to meet only with everyone together for worship, which included singing, preaching, and prayer. Sunday Schools began as an extra class on Sundays before or after church, to attract children from homes of non-Christian families to attend church, in order to teach them Bible lessons. Some thought this would be a distraction from the purpose of the church to worship.

2    Biblically speaking, when God sends revival, He is converting large numbers of lost people and strengthening everyone's commitment to the Lord with an abundant outpouring of His grace.

3    The point is, just as God can bring enormous difficulties and obstacles to an end, no matter how impossible they seem to be, so He can get us through extremely difficult problems too, even ones that seem to have no possible solution. All He requires of us is that we trust and obey Him. He overcame impossible obstacles for the Israelites even when they were not obedient! How much more is He willing to do when we are?

# Chapter Fifteen:
## SUSAN BECOMES A BELIEVER

1 Why do people have to first recognize that "I am a great sinner," as Susan did, before they turn to Christ as their Savior? (page 106)

2 When we feel weak and unable, but still go ahead and speak out for the Lord and witness, He gives strength in the process. Have you ever felt anything like that from Him? (page 107)

3 The author seems very worried about "keeping the Sabbath," and there are some Christians who believe that it is against God's Law for anyone to work on that day. Is this something we should still be thinking about today?

4 At the end of the story, witnessing has become very important to Charles. What would it take in your life, for you to become passionate and frequent in sharing about Jesus with unsaved people?

## Memory Verse
### Matthew 28:18-19

"All authority in heaven and on earth has been given to me. Go therefore and make disciples of all nations...." (ESV)

"All power is given unto me in heaven and in earth. Go ye therefore, and teach all nations..." (KJV)

*On this memory verse, consider memorizing from verse 18 all the way through the end of verse 20, if you can.*

1. As Matthew 1:21 tells us, Jesus has come to save His people from their sins. If we don't see that we are sinful, there is no hope of us coming to Him for the very salvation we need more than anything else!

2. Talk with your child about times when you have been aware that the Lord has given you surprising wisdom, insight, or boldness to speak that you did not naturally or personally have. Find out if the Lord has done this for your child already too! This should make for some very encouraging conversation.

3. A more Biblical way to think about the Sabbath is this: God gave a day of Sabbath rest to the nation of Israel; but now we should understand that the Sabbath day rest was a pointer to Jesus Christ, to show us that we must rest from our works in Him, and trust that the work He did is what saves us. Still, many who think we should "keep the Sabbath" are mainly concerned that Christians not neglect going to church, which is a valid concern. If people feel obligated to not work on Sunday and devote the whole day to the Lord, our Lord sees that as an honorable act of worship.

4. Let this final question, and the close of the story, bring you to talk with your child about times in your life when you were lazy, cowardly, or for some reason slow or reluctant to witness to people; and what events, if any, made you become more zealous, bold, and ready to obey the Great Commission? Then talk about Philippians 2:14-15 and 1 Peter 3:15.

## Activities

1. Write out some of the most meaningful Scriptures you have memorized as a result of this book. If you can think of one that would be valuable to share with a friend, find a way to do that in a letter.

2. Is there an orphanage near you, or even a home for disabled children, or a children's hospital? Make a visit to one of the needy children in such a place, to show them compassion, and think of something nice you could do for them. What would you want someone to do for you, if you were stuck in such a place?

3. The next time you're at church and the Lord's Supper is being passed around, don't allow yourself to merely sit there, thinking about other things, or nothing at all; least of all, to get bored while waiting for this portion of the meeting to end! Try picking up your Bible and reading some verses about the death of Jesus and what it accomplished. Or, even look in the back of your hymnal (if your church has those, or the lyrics to songs printed in a bulletin) for songs about the cross of Christ and let them help you meditate on it.

# THE REWARD OF CHILDHOOD TRUTH
## Study Guide

Life will bring you daily situations in which you will be either learning to be honest and tell the truth, or you will become skilled at covering up your actions with lies. Everyone who has chosen the truthful path found life pleasant, and everyone who has ever chosen the lying path ended up miserable. In these two stories, we learn of two boys who told the truth when others suspected them of being liars; and a little girl who people expected to be truthful, who instead tried to get away with a lie! Lies will always be regretted later, but those who tell the truth have no regrets and know that they have honored the God of truth and will not incur His wrath.

# Chapter 1:
# TRUTH ON TRIAL

1  Some parents always take their children's side, whether they have done right or wrong. Are your parents like that? Were you ever happy that they defended you and stood on your side when you were clearly wrong?

2  Why does Mr. Arnold call the plant his Prodigium Mundi?

3  Mr. Benson shows wisdom by ceasing to argue with Mr. Arnold. Why do we know that it was wise to quit arguing? (page 5)

4  Have you ever been accused of lying when you definitely told the truth? How did that feel? What did you do about it?

## Memory Verse

### Ephesians 4:25

"Therefore, having put away falsehood, let each one of you speak the truth with his neighbor; for we are members one of another." (ESV)

"Wherefore putting away lying, speak every man truth with his neighbor: for we are members one of another." (KJV)

## Answers for Chapter 1:

1   This could lead to some uncomfortable discussion; be prayerfully honest about it, in case some occasion in which you were unwise or wrongly biased in favor of your child comes up. Some children will admit this, some never will. But since this is a story about honesty and truthfulness, this is one of the most intense opportunities to test the depth and genuineness of that honesty.

2   All plants have Latin names that are used in science textbooks. Some people like to use those Latin names rather than the more common English names for their plants.

3   There are times when it is futile to continue arguing with someone; they are incorrigible (meaning, they won't change, even if proven wrong). It can even become a foolish enterprise to try.

4   Since parents and other authorities in children's lives do not know everything, like God, most children will, at some time, have the experience of not being believed when they told the truth. Talk this through with your child. Show them that, sometimes when you are not believed, the only thing you can do is to keep proving by your character that you are not a liar. Eventually people will accept the fact that you are a truthful person.

# Chapter 2:
## THE TRUTH IS TOLD

1. Why do you think Mr. Arnold was angry and upset when Mr. Benson offered to pay for the damaged plant, rather than welcoming the offer? (page 17)

2. Why will people sometimes "live and thrive" on their sufferings, the wrongs done against them, and "hug it to their hearts," as page 18 says Mr. Arnold was doing?

3. How would understanding 1 Corinthians 6:19-20 have helped Mr. Arnold? (page 19) "Or do you not know that your body is a temple of the Holy Spirit within you, whom you have from God? You are not your own, for you were bought with a price. So glorify God in your body."

## Memory Verse
### Proverbs 16:18

"Pride goes before destruction, and a haughty spirit before a fall." (ESV)

"Pride goeth before destruction, and an haughty spirit before a fall." (KJV)

1   He was a prideful man, feeling self-sufficient that he had enough money to buy another one himself; but mostly he was displeased and annoyed that he was wrong about the boys being dishonest. He was resentful about being mistaken about them. He would rather they had been proven to be liars! And the story also tells us he was still irritated about the plant. Don't ever let yourself become a person like this, who finds it so hard to get over a wrong committed against you!

2   It makes people feel important at times to have some wrong they have suffered; and they also are reluctant to give up their grudge, because then they will have to give up their reasons for resentment.

3   Once a person learns and accepts that his whole life is supposed to be glorifying to God, right down to every deed we do with our bodies, then we will see how foolish it is to make a fuss over minor things – such as a broken plant! Serving God is too important to be fussy about such trivialities.

# Chapter 3:
# THE TRUTH IS REWARDED

1   Why do you think living only for making and saving lots of money is so unsatisfying, even though you do end up very rich?

2   The idea of being "surety" for someone else — what is it, and does the Bible really forbid it?

3   Think of a time when truthfulness brought some rewards your way.

## Memory Verse

### 1 Timothy 6:9

"But those who desire to be rich fall into temptation, into a snare, into many senseless and harmful desires that plunge people into ruin and destruction." (ESV)

"But they that will be rich fall into temptation and a snare, and into many foolish and hurtful lusts, which drown men in destruction and perdition." (KJV)

1   When a person is obsessed with getting and keeping lots of money, it fills his mind with all sorts of pains and agonies. It causes more suffering than it is worth. These kinds of strong desires destroy a person from the inside. See 1 Timothy 6:9-10: "But those who desire to be rich fall into temptation, into a snare, into many senseless and harmful desires that plunge people into ruin and destruction. For the love of money is a root of all kinds of evils. It is through this craving that some have wandered away from the faith and pierced themselves with many pangs."

2   The answer is yes, or at the very least, the Bible strongly discourages it on the basis that it's very unwise, because it puts us in bondage to others. (More recent Bible versions will call this "security" or "pledge"). See Proverbs 17:18 and 22:26.

Proverbs 11:15 says, "Whoever puts up a security for a stranger will surely suffer harm, but he who hates striking hands in pledge is secure."

These verses show us that the reason being surety (old word for it) or security (the newer word for it) is making yourself responsible for someone else's debt, and becoming obligated to it by a contract or even a handshake (what the Proverb called "striking hands").

3   Hopefully there will be more than one time! Maybe you can think of several.

# Chapter 4:
# A FRIENDSHIP GROWS

1    Is it sinful to be suspicious of people, as Mr. Arnold confesses he was? Always expecting the worst from them.

2    Explain why he is correct when he says (on page 46) that "there is no virtue without truth."

3    Why does hearing of other people's deaths sometimes have a good influence on our character? (page 47)

4    If we learn to think as Mr. Arnold does by the end of the story, who has blessed us more – those who bless us in financial ways, or those who bless us with spiritual truths?

## Memory Verse

### Proverbs 12:19

"Truthful lips endure forever, but a lying tongue is but for a moment." (ESV)

"The lip of truth shall be established for ever: but a lying tongue is but for a moment." (KJV)

1   Yes, it is sinful, because love is supposed to try to believe the best we reasonably can about people, and hopes (1 Cor. 13:7). We cannot be thinking right if we are always suspecting people of doing us wrong.

2   One of the most basic attributes of a person who is righteous is to be truthful; those who lie always have something evil to cover up, and so they cannot be doing right.

3   It makes people take eternity seriously and realize that we do all have to face God.

4   Surely your child will see by the end of this story that, it is far greater to be blessed with spiritual truths than with any amount of worldly goods. Because, as Jesus said, "For what does it profit a man to gain the whole world and forfeit his soul?" (Mark 8;36)

# Chapter 1:
# LISTENING TO SATAN'S DECEITFUL VOICE

1 What should Mary have done when her brother tried to get her to participate in his lie?

2 What does it show about our hearts and state of mind, when we can tell a lie with "boldness and readiness" (swiftly), as page 57 mentions they did?

3 Mary tried to soothe her conscience about not confessing this lie, by telling herself she would never tell another. But why is this an inadequate way to solve what she did?

4 Every lie we tell tends to lead us to tell more lies. Why is that, do you think?

## Memory Verse

### Psalm 120:2

"Deliver me, O Lord, from lying lips, from a deceitful tongue." (ESV)

"Deliver my soul, O Lord, from lying lips, and from a deceitful tongue." (KJV)

## Answers for Chapter 1:

1   We should never let anyone persuade us to join them in a lie. Turn the tables on them and urge them to be truthful. You can remind them of how displeased God is with liars, and also that He is committed to both expose them and destroy them in the end, if they persist in that habit.

2   It shows that a person is in bondage or slavery to sin if they have reached a point of boldly and swiftly telling lies; it also shows a hard heart and a seared conscience. (see Ephesians 4:18 and 1 Timothy 4:2)

3   We cannot undo the guilt of our sins by not doing it again. Resolve to not to do a sinful thing again can be an act of repentance; but real resolve not only turns from sin, but confesses past sin too. If we are serious about resisting our sins, we will accept that we need help from others to win the battle. Confessing to them and seeking their help is a way of being serious about fighting sin.

4   Because when we lie, we have something to cover up. The truth tends to come out in time, and if we are determined to prevent that from uncovering our lie, we end up finding it necessary to make up more lies to cover our tracks.

# Chapter 2:
# MARY'S SCARRED CONSCIENCE

1  Are we doing others any favor, when we help them continue to cover their lies and not suffer the consequences of telling the truth – or do we do them more harm that way?

2  Have you ever resolved to undo some sin you committed, making things right, or confess some sin you had hidden, but then before the time came to do it, you reconsidered and went back on your decision? Why did this happen?

3  Feeling deeply guilty and ashamed of your sin is a heavy-hearted, miserable way to live. What simple act can keep us from being enslaved to this misery? See Psalm 32:3-5.

## Memory Verse

### 1 John 1:9

"If we confess our sins, He is faithful and just to forgive us our sins, and to cleanse us from all unrighteousness." (ESV)

"If we confess our sins, He is faithful and just to forgive us our sins, and to cleanse us from all unrighteousness." (KJV)

1   I think we know that we do people great harm if we let them get away with lies. It may make us feel merciful when we shield others from the consequences of coming clean with the truth. But we are only preventing temporary suffering while doing nothing to alleviate the fact that they will suffer God's judgment.

2   The Bible calls this being "double-minded" – we waver back and forth from a resolve to do what's right to settling for a sinful choice. It shows that we are weak and in need of the power of the Holy Spirit.

3   If we will confess our sins to God, without making excuses, He is willing to forgive our guilt completely, so that we do not have to live under the crushing burden of it anymore!

# Chapter 3:
# CONFESS YOUR FAULTS ONE TO ANOTHER

1   Why is it necessary for us to confess our sins to one another, as well as to God?

2   What is the conscience and what does the Word of God tell us about it? (Use a concordance to find the places where "conscience" is found in the Bible. You will find it comes up about 32 times.)

3   Why would someone write out a confession of their sin at times, as Mary did on page 70, instead of just talking about it to her parents? Is there some advantage to doing it this way?

## Memory Verse

### James 5:16

"Therefore, confess your sins to one another, and pray for one another, that you may be healed." (ESV)

"Confess your faults one to another, and pray one for another, that ye may be healed." (KJV)

1  It sounds like enough to confess our sins to God, but James 5:16 says to confess them to one another, too. And many godly examples in the Scriptures show people confessing their sins to other godly people. This is how we recruit help!

2  What you will find in the Scriptures primarily is that our conscience judges us, reminding us of what we know in our thoughts. It will either make us feel right in our actions or condemned in our actions.

3  Writing out our words of confession of sin will make precise and accurate, exactly what we really said in our confession. Sometimes that's very important, so we know what we mean.

Also, it can help the person confessing sort out their thoughts and words clearly, especially after they have delayed doing what ought to have been done a long time ago, which may have confused their thinking.

## Activities

1  Do you have a neighbor who is grumpy or grouchy? Maybe he is suspicious of you or just plain doesn't like people. Well, we all have some sin or another in our heart. How about you think of some surprising act of kindness you could do for that neighbor? Take them some cookies, offer to rake the leaves in his yard, or think up something else. (Do not go on his property without his permission, that may arouse his suspicion or make him angry – but pray about and think up something nice you can do for them!)

2  Sometime when your family is praying together, if you have never done this before, try it now: don't just pray about things that you want or blessings for other people. Confess one of your sins (it doesn't have to be some big secret – even one of the sins that members in your family already know you do or have, like having a temper or not always showing a cheerful and willing spirit to help with work).

# ROSES AND THORNS
## Study Guide

There are several stories built into and around one key idea in the book, all told by Aunt Eleanor to her niece and nephew. Aunt Eleanor is skillful at using stories to encourage children to be honest, kind, peaceful and content.

# Chapter 1:
# THOUGHTFUL JAN AND CARELESS KITTY

1   In what ways are love, joy, and peace to be compared with flowers? And in what way is it right to compare hatred, bitterness, revenge, and envy, for instance, to thorns that cut and pierce us?

2   Page 5 says "Thoughtlessness brings about more trouble than willful intentions do." Do you think that is true, and how so?

3   Why was it not wise to go to the meeting?

## Memory Verse

### Proverbs 13:20

"Whoever walks with the wise will become wise, but the companion of fools will suffer harm." (ESV)

"He that walketh with wise men shall be wise; but a companion of fools shall be destroyed." (KJV)

1  Love, joy, and peace are beautiful traits which bring happiness to people, both to be around and even to see in others. They are fruitful – they grow by the nourishing of the Spirit who is like living water. But hatred, bitterness, revenge and envy wound people and bring great pain into human relationships.

2  It may be doubtful that thoughtlessness causes more trouble than intentional evil does; but we must accept the fact that thoughtlessness can be responsible for an awful lot of trouble in the world. It also happens a lot more often than flat-out evil actions, and so may well cause more trouble and pain, by its frequency.

3  It was only for pretense that people were going to look for other jobs; actually many of them went there to have a wild party and engage in foolish behavior.

*Definition*

LOVE

---

Caring sacrificially for others just as
much as you take care of yourself.

# Chapter 2:
# THE POOR WEAVER

1  Do you think it is possible for you to make very little pay and still be happy? How would you attain that?

2  The Bible tells us that people with a hot temper cause harm to others. How have you found them harmful, or what harm do you think they cause?

3  How is God able to make bad events work together for good, as the promise in Romans 8:28 says He does?

*Memory Verse*

**Proverbs 15:16**

"Better is a little with the fear of the Lord, than great treasure and trouble with it." (ESV)

"Better is little with the fear of the Lord, than great treasure and trouble therewith." (KJV)

1. Having the attitudes of 1 Timothy 6:6-8 is part of the answer. Be content having enough to meet your needs, and don't get greedy to have more than you need!

2. Here are some Scriptures about this subject to look up and talk about. They will lead you to some very definite conclusions: Proverbs 14:17, 14:29, 15:18

3. For one, because He is all-wise, can foresee all events and has things planned, even events which look to us to be entirely bad can be designed to bring about a better and higher good; further, because He is all-powerful, He can turn the worst events into a blessing. Many stories are told in Scripture of God taking an awful situation and turning it around for good. The most notable instance of this is, when evil men conspired to murder Jesus, His Son, God had it all planned in order to bless the world by making atonement for our sin! (Acts 2:22-24 and Acts 4:27-28). Also see Genesis 50:17-21 as the outcome of the story of Joseph's miseries.

## Activity

Begin a thankful journal!
A place to write down things, events,
blessings that you are thankful for.
So you have something to read at times when
you are discouraged, to help you remember
the wonderful things God has done!

## Definition

### CONTENTMENT

Living satisfied with knowing that God has given me everything that I need, and even many of the things that I want.

# Chapter 3:
## THE THREE BROTHERS

1   What do you suppose God thinks of those who incite war between other people, for their own gain, as Robert did?

2   How would the fear of God have prevented Robert and Roger from engaging in the types of business they did?

3   Could you have joy in the Lord if you were captured by slave-traders and forced into servitude, as Randal had been? Of, if you were poor and honest, but your brothers were rich and dishonest – how would you be able to find the power to be joyful in the Lord?

## Memory Verse

### Proverbs 19:23

"The fear of the Lord leads to life, and whoever has it rests satisfied; he will not be visited by harm." (ESV)

"The fear of the Lord tendeth to life, and he that hath it shall abide satisfied; he shall not be visited with evil." (KJV)

1    God is very angry with those who cause strife and conflict between people. Look at the kinds of things that it is compared to in Proverbs 6:16-19!

2    When we fear God (that is, respect Him above all else, and know that He has more power to bring consequences upon us for our deeds than anyone else), then it makes us think about whether we are pleasing Him. We would rather lose some of the gains we have in the world than disobey Him!

3    Joy in the Lord is one of those things which is poorly understood. Do not make your child feel as if he would be obliged to be happy all the way around, even if he was in captivity or in some other miserable circumstances. But rather, even when we are in a terrible situation or miseries, we can still have joy over what the Lord has done for us: if for no other reason than that, He will save us from it eventually and take us home to Himself! Whatever we are going through is not all there is, and it will not end up that way.

## Activity

Pray for the persecuted church
and those in prison for the faith.
The word is full of tyrannical govern-
ments and cruel dictators who hate
the gospel of Christ.

# Chapter 4:
# CARELESS WORDS

1 Sometimes children in the past were put in "boarding schools." Do you think such schools were a good or bad idea for Christian parents to send their children to?

2 In this chapter, Nell was certainly persuasively made aware of the many sins of her tongue. Have you ever had someone point out your sins in a way that was anything like that? But look at how Nell responded on page 30.

## Memory Verse

### Proverbs 27:6

"Faithful are the wounds of a friend; profuse are the kisses of an enemy." (ESV)

"Faithful are the wounds of a friend, but the kisses of an enemy are deceitful." (KJV)

1   Many missionaries think that boarding schools are a necessity for their children, but others regard them as not necessarily wise. While some parents send their children to such a school at a young age, this can easily turn into neglect of their responsibility to raise their own children. Some do this so that they can feel safer preaching the gospel in a hostile culture, on the mission field, without their children being there, among the cultural dangers. It is the author's position that it would always be better for parents to be with their own children, regardless of other factors.

2   Just walk with your child through an honest discussion of how frank Nell's friend Leah was with Nell, and how humbly Nell responded to it all. Don't let the conversation be only about your child; let him or her learn that you also have not always appreciated correction nor received it with a humble and welcoming spirit.

# Chapter 5:
# THE LOST CHILDREN

1    Why did it trouble Maggie in her heart to have traveled as far as Muddy Run, when she had been told not to go to the mountain? (page 36)

2    Why did Maggie fear (on page 38) that God would not let her go home again?

## Memory Verse

### Psalm 103:10

"He does not deal with us according to our sins, nor repay us according to our iniquities." (ESV)

"He hath not dealt with us after our sins; nor rewarded us according to our iniquities." (KJV)

1  As page 36 tells us, she knew that the intent of her mother's instruction had been, to prevent them from going too far and getting lost or being exposed to danger. Never justify your actions by keeping only the precise words of the rule someone gives you, while ignoring what you know to be the intent of it.

2  We often do not realize the extent of the goodness of God, that He does not punish us as our actions deserve. Frequently He continues being good to us, even though we have earned His punishment. He is better than that!

*Definition*

OBEDIENCE

---

Doing what is expected of me
cheerfully, immediately,
and thoroughly.

*from* Kids of Character Bible Study, *by Marilyn Boyer, page 131*

# Chapter 6:
# THE THUNDERSTORM

1   Why does this chapter picture going to Jesus Christ as like running into a shelter?

2   Have you ever been afraid of thunderstorms? If you haven't been, what would you say to help someone else who was?

## Memory Verse

### Proverbs 18:10

"The name of the Lord is a strong tower; the righteous man runs into it and is safe." (ESV)

"The name of the Lord is a strong tower; the righteous runneth into it, and is safe." (KJV)

1   Frequently, the Word of God depicts our relationship to God as one of hiding in the protection of a shelter: Psalm 61:4, 91:1 for instance. It has to do with how He shields us from troubles, by giving us someone to run to and rely upon.

2   Talk this through with your children thoughtfully, and help them learn both that God is in full control over the storms, and if they do not experience these fears, to have compassion on those who do.

# PRISON ROSES

*This brief portion of the book is a story of its own.*

1  Martha encouraged herself by saying, "If it is God's will, something will come out in the trial to prove that I am innocent." (page 54) Can you think of a time when you were innocent, and not guilty of something you were accused of, yet you accepted that you would have to wait on the Lord to prove your innocence to others in time?

2  Just as remarkable as that is the next sentence on the same page (54), that Martha is also able to "bless Him (God)" even from prison!? What would it take for you to be able to suffer time in prison and still give thanks to God?

3  How did Martha end up being proven innocent and getting set free?

## Memory Verse

### 1 Peter 2:23

"When He was reviled, He did not revile in return; when He suffered, He did not threaten, but continued entrusting Himself to Him who judges righteously." (ESV)

"Who, when He was reviled, reviled not again; when He suffered, He threatened not, but committed Himself to Him that judgeth righteously." (KJV)

1   Your child will likely very easily understand how hard it is to wait for God to vindicate you (prove you innocent) when others are considering you guilty. Help your child learn what it might be like to wait on God to do it, while you patiently wait.

2   Your child may or may not find it in himself to be able to do this; but point out how godly people, down through history, have suffered prison sentences, and yet been able to praise God from prison (Acts 16:25 – the Apostle Paul and Silas), or even to give thanks for certain aspects of the circumstances. Martha was thankful that she could read quietly, do her knitting hobby, and most of all that she was not in a "common room" (one big cell, containing lots of prisoners) where she would have to bear with all the hateful and cursing speech of a crowd of corrupt men.

3   The answer is in the middle of page 59: Mr. Dawes and his urging for a more full investigation, resulted in the two men who had really committed the robbery being discovered; once their secret plot began to unravel, they admitted the burglarly. This was a great act of the mercy of God, because often men will not confess their sins, even when evidence against them becomes overwhelming.

Another excellent story on this topic is entitled *The Basket of Flowers,* also available from Grace & Truth Books.

# TAMPERING WITH TEMPTATION
## Study Guide

This book contains three stories, not just one. The first story, about Young Martin, is about a boy who was first careless and later dishonest about the handling of his employer's money. The second story, *Farmer Goodwin's Rule,* is a brief but powerful one about not backing down from doing what you know is right, even when it's challenging and costs you. And the third story, about Albert and Herbert, shows us that we must be courageous and willing to say "No," even when others pressure us to say "Yes" to their worldly and sinful pleasures.

# YOUNG MARTIN AND THE SILVER SIXPENCE

1   Is punishment for a "trifling dishonesty" wrong of parents to do, or does a child benefit from it?

2   Each time you see a dime or quarter on the ground, does being honest require you try to find who-ever lost it? If not, why not?

3   Once Bernard learned who (Lorimer) had lost the coin, why was it wrong for him not to admit he had it and give it to him? Page 8

4   Do you think Mr. Bender was too strict in his judgment of Martin for not having accounting books agree precisely with the amount collected? Page 10

5   "Was he all right?", is asked on page 17. Martin's reputation was not damaged. His money was not damaged. What is damaged?

## Memory Verse

### James 1:14

"But each person is tempted when he is lured and enticed by his own desire." (ESV)

"But every man is tempted, when he is drawn away of his own lust and enticed." (KJV)

1   It is good for parents to punish small acts of dishonesty, because if we learn to sin in small ways and get away with it, we will move from bad to worse, and gain boldness to commit much more serious sins. We must learn that "he who is faithful in little will be faithful in much, and he who is unfaithful in little will be unfaithful in much."

2   If we merely find a coin outside, we may not have any obligation to look for who lost it. That would be a thoughtful (but not required or necessary) gesture. We must keep in mind that, in the time of this story, a sixpence would have the value of many dollars today. Even a coin was worth much more in those times. It might have been equivalent to a whole day's work. If we found that much money outside (like a $100 bill, or a big wad of bills that fell from someone's pocket), it would be much more serious and we probably would try to see who had lost it.

3   Because now he knew to whom the coin truly belonged. There was no excuse for him keeping it any longer at all. Also, he justified this keeping it by convincing himself that Lorimer did not need it. You see, the real meaning of the phrase on page 8 is not what we think:

"Lorimer does not want the money, and I do" – The word *want* in this sentence means *need*, as in many English books from over 100 years ago.

4   Not at all. You will find, when you get a job, that if you are collecting money, anyone you work for will want the numbers to match exactly: what you have recorded will always be expected to be what you collected.

5   His conscience and his heart are what has been damaged!

A key, main point of this story appears on page 18: Speaking of people who had known Bernard for a long time, it says, ""They thought his ruin was a sudden temptation too powerful for him to resist. Alas! They did not know how the temptation came first in a way that the lad could have easily resisted. Instead, he had tampered with the chain of temptation until that chain was strengthened."

In light of this, be sure to finish the discussion of this section by making clear that sinful choices are often made by gradual degrees; and each time we indulge in one, we make it easier and more likely that we will do wrong the next time. Our mind, heart, and conscience become scarred and get hardened. So: remember often to pray as we are taught in The Lord's Prayer: "Lead us not into temptation, but deliver us from evil." (Matthew 6:13)

# FARMER GOODWIN'S RULE

1   What does Farmer Goodwin's rule make you think of? The rule is:

"Never do anything during the day that will cause you to worry at night."

2   Have you ever felt embarrassed that someone would see you reading the Bible? Most Christians have felt that way at times. Why do we feel this way?

3   What is wrong with our thinking when we say "No one will ever know" as a way of encouraging ourselves to commit sin?

## Memory Verse

### Matthew 10:32

"So everyone who acknowledges me before men, I also will acknowledge before my Father who is in heaven, but whoever denies me before men, I also will deny before my Father who is in heaven." (ESV)

"Whosoever therefore shall confess me before men, him will I confess also before my Father which is in heaven. But whosoever shall deny me before men, him will I also deny before my Father which is in heaven." (KJV)

1   Most of us do some thinking at night, when we are alone in bed; it's normal for us to reflect on our day then, and sometimes we ask ourselves in the quietness, if we have been doing the right thing or not. You see, by "worry," Farmer Goodwin means, when the memory of what you did during the day grieves you or causes you to feel regrets about it.

2   We all want to be liked, and we know there are people who think it is weird of us to read the Bible. We do not like people to think we are odd. But we must get over that and be courageous, to stand for honoring the Lord by honoring His Word, no matter what people think about us! In fact, we should make them to feel that they are the wrong ones for not loving God's Word.

3   It shows that we fear people but do not fear God. And He already knows all of our sins! So it is foolishness to fear men rather than Him.

## Activity

Taking this book as a whole (both stories), think about a time when you found something that didn't belong to you, or the wrong change was given back to you for a purchase. How did you handle that moment? If you were honest, how did the other person react?

## Definition

### COURAGE

Being willing to stand alone
for what is right while entrusting
my fears to God's care.

# Chapter 1:
# ALFRED AND HERBERT: WHO IS A COWARD?

1  What do you think it means, that we will give account of every idle word in the day of judgment? (page 51)

2  Page 53: What does it mean to "swear not at all"?

## Memory Verse

### Proverbs 15:3

"The eyes of the Lord are in every place, keeping watch on the evil and the good." (ESV)

"The eyes of the Lord are in every place, beholding the evil and the good." (KJV)

1. It certainly means that nothing escapes the eye of God. He sees everything we do, hears everything we say, and He has complete rights to bring up anything He wants to on the judgment day.

2. It does not mean, refrain from bad language (even though that comes up in other places in the story). It means that, when you make a promise, don't try to make others take it more seriously by saying it more strongly or in the name of something. Just make a promise and keep it.

Still, there are valid lessons to learn about our language here: If your children are not familiar with blasphemy, curse words, using God's name in vain, you decide when (at what age, for instance) to have a judicious and careful conversation with them about these subjects.

*Definition*

**SELF-CONTROL**

Subjecting my own desires to
the control of the Holy Spirit.

# Chapter 2:
# THE FALL

1 You will find many older books condemn all going to the theater. Most of the reason was, many of the stage shows were quite full of immorality. Do you ever watch TV shows that you should not permit your eyes to see?

Also make clear to your child that (page 61) shows that their theater attendance also involved a lot of heavy alcohol drinking (enough to leave them with a headache or a hangover) and involved a lot of irresponsible spending of money he could not really afford.

2 What do you think they are talking about in this topic of Sabbath-breaking? They were very concerned that people not neglect church and engage in other sports and entertainments at times when they could and should be worshiping. What does your family do?

3 What did getting drunk result in for Herbert?

## Memory Verse

### 1 Corinthians 10:12

"Therefore let anyone who thinks that he stands take heed lest he fall." (ESV)

"Let him that thinketh he stand take heed lest he fall." (KJV)

1   Discuss this topic with your child, and apply this honestly and thoughtfully to your family's TV watching. We Christians so commonly watch TV and go to movies, we tend to not take seriously books from long ago that condemn worldly entertainment, and quickly dismiss them as legalistic. It could be we are very wrong and being much too careless!

2   Another controversial topic is found here: You can see that Sabbath-breaking is a big deal in this story. Some Christians still believe that Sunday is the Sabbath day, and the commandment of Exodus 20 to rest from work and worldly entertainments on that special day of worship must still be obeyed. Others believe that Christ fulfills the Sabbath command and that the way we "keep" the Sabbath is by resting from our good works in Him. But either way, all Christians believe that we should not neglect worship with the church, and doing other things instead. So keep that in mind as you read this chapter.

3   He was confused and his judgment was distorted. He could not remember events well, and he was not as good a worker. You do not want to be indulging in alcohol! It has this effect on the mind and

## Activities

1   Can you think of someone you have been not entirely honest with about something in the past, and to whom maybe you owe a confession of that?

2   Is there someone who tried to get you to do wrong, and you were cowardly about it and went along? Can you find the courage to write them a letter or talk to them about how wrong you were to succumb and ask them to repent, too?

# THEOBOLD THE IRON-HEARTED
## Study Guide

It's one thing when two knights from opposing armies meet on the battlefield. They must serve their kings and fight to the death! But how about when those same two knights meet, and one of them is in dire need of medical help and assistance? Would you take advantage of his weakness and end his life, or would you show mercy? These decisions are not easy to make. Discover how the gospel of Jesus is really the most important thing in all of life, after all, and if you ever have an opportunity to explain it, even to an enemy – even an enemy who hates you for that very message! – that you ought to prayerfully do so.

# Chapter 1:
# THE WOUNDED KNIGHT

The wars to which the opening of this chapter refers were known as the Hussite wars, which followed the tragic and wicked execution of John Huss.

Find the city of Prague on a map. It is currently (as of 2016) the capitol city of the Czech Republic.

John Huss (1369-1415) is sometimes named in history as Jan Hus, or John Hus. He is considered an important forerunner to the Protestant Reformation, as he preached against many heresies, abuses, and unbiblical practices in the Roman Catholic Church. He had a profound influence on many in Europe, but was burned at the stake by order of the Pope in 1415. Those who followed his teachings became far more numerous after his execution than before.

1   How should we feel or handle it, if a Christian man is killed in a battle by enemy soldiers, fighting for the evil side? Do we have to despair or wonder why a good God allowed it?

2   What would you consider your duty to a wounded soldier, if you found one?

## Memory Verse

### Luke 6:35

"But love your enemies, and do good, and lend, expecting nothing in return, and your reward will be great, and you will be sons of the Most High, for he is kind to the ungrateful and the evil." (ESV)

"But love ye your enemies, and do good, and lend, hoping for nothing again; and your reward shall be great, and ye shall be the children of the Highest: for he is kind unto the unthankful and to the evil." (KJV)

1   We need not despair, never grieving like unsaved people who have no hope (1 Thess. 4:13). Rather, we can feel a peace that, the Lord knew this would happen; He has His own purposes (everyone has a time to die, in God's plan); and we need not despair or wonder about God's goodness, because He knows what He is doing. Besides, in the case of a godly man, the Lord has taken him home to heaven!

2   Finding a wounded soldier, even from the enemy side, gives us an opportunity to love an enemy, which the Bible tells us to do.

Note: The book, *A Cup of Cold Water: The Compassion of Nurse Edith Cavell* is another valuable biographical story about a wartime nurse who cared for wounded soldiers on both sides of the conflict, at great risk to herself. Also available through Grace and Truth Books.

# Chapter 2:
## AN ENEMY TREATED KINDLY

1   What were the words that indicated to Erik that this wounded soldier was fighting for the enemy's side?

2   Now that you know this soldier is from the enemy army, would your thoughts be different about helping him than they were when you finished reading chapter one?

3   Would you pray for the healing of a wounded enemy soldier, or for his death?

4   What "Holy Church" did the wounded knight mean at the bottom of page 9? How would you answer his question, as to whether Christians could fight against "the Church," as he thought of it?

5   When you think of Islamic terrorist groups today who invade and slaughter Christian people in their towns and homes, are you able to have compassion on them in their blindness and bondage to sinful hatred, as well as to the people they harm?

## Memory Verse

### Proverbs 24:17

"Do not rejoice when your enemy falls, and let not your heart be glad when he stumbles." (ESV)

"Rejoice not when thine enemy falleth, and let not thine heart be glad when he stumbleth" (KJV)

1    When he heard the man say, "May the Holy Virgin repay you" (page 9). Also the appearance of his shield, the same page tells us, which means it had some symbol on it indicating the enemy side.

2    This will be a difficult question for some children, as many will feel as if loyalty to their own side will require enmity to the other side, under all circumstances. This makes a good opportunity to convey to your child that, it has been the policy of many nations to treat their prisoners from the opposing side – especially the wounded – with kindness.

3    Be prepared to discuss with your child that there may be one more than righteous way to pray about this. Probably the best prayer would be to pray for his conversion to Christ, and for him to live so that he might be saved. But if a child concludes he should pray for his death, so that he no longer makes war against and slaughters the innocent, that can be valid too. There are a variety of Psalms in which King David prays for the death of the wicked.

4    The wounded knight was referring to The Holy Roman Catholic Church, as it was commonly called in those times. However, there has never been anything "Holy" about the Catholic Church, but rather it has been a bastion of idolatry for centuries, and a persecutor of those in the true faith.

A godly answer to his challenging question, "But are they Christians who despise and fight the Holy Church?", would be to ask him, "On what basis do you think of the Roman Catholic Church as 'holy,' when it follows not the Word of God, but the traditions and teachings of men, and has opposed and persecuted, for centuries, all who point that out to them?"

5    It is reasonable and biblical to have mixed feelings when it comes to the violent acts of men against innocent people, desires for both justice and for mercy. So don't feel bad if you desire to see Islamic terrorists defeated by the military, or stopped by means of prison or death. These are all part of understanding and valuing the intervening judgment of God and are a godly response. Yet it is also a godly response to desire them to learn of the grace of God and to find salvation in Christ.

# Chapter 3:
# LOVE YOUR ENEMIES

1  Who are the Hussites and Calixtans? (page 14)

2  Who are the Taborites? (page 17)

3  Why is Jesus named The Prince of Peace in this story?

4  Theobold speaks of committing blasphemy against The Holy Church. There is a serious error in his thinking. What is it?

## Memory Verse

### Colossians 3:15

"And let the peace of Christ rule in your hearts, to which indeed you were called in one body. And be thankful." (ESV)

"And let the peace of God rule in your hearts, to the which also are ye called in one body; and be ye thankful." (KJV)

1   The Hussites were a Christian movement in the kingdom of Bohemia, whose leader was the Czech reformer, Jan Hus (sometimes known as John Huss). He was a forerunner of the Protestant Great Reformation.

The Calixtans are a group we know much less about, except that they were disciples who practiced both believer's baptism (as opposed to infant baptism) and who would allow all their Christian members to partake of both the wine and the bread in the Lord's Supper. The Catholic Church resisted them as rebels, believing it was wrong to allow anyone but the priest to partake of the wine (what most churches would use is grape juice today).

2   The Taborites were also Christians of Bohemia, mostly who worked in mines and were poor. They likewise resisted the Catholic church, particularly for its gaudy wealth, and they lived a simple life-style.

3   Christ is called "The Prince of Peace," for one, because it is a biblical title for Him (Isaiah 9:6); but also in the story at this point because, the point is, Christ does not conquer men by human violence, but rather by bringing gospel peace and love into their hearts.

4   Blasphemy is committed against God. We cannot blaspheme "the church." He had too high a regard for the opinions of his church. Sometimes churches can be wrong, and it is not blasphemy at all to disagree with them; rather, we are to always faithfully call our churches back to conformity to the Word of God.

# Chapter 4:
# THE LION RETURNS

1 How would you be able to have love and compassion for enemies, who killed those who are dear to you, as Erik was able to and urged Franz to do?

2 What does it mean that we who believe in Christ could bear the image of God? (page 27)

3 What is the difference between thinking we can earn a right to God's love, and receiving His love purely by grace? Explain it in your own words.

## Memory Verse

### Romans 5:8

"But God shows His love for us in that while we were still sinners, Christ died for us." (ESV)

"But God commendeth His love toward us, in that, while we were yet sinners, Christ died for us." (KJV)

1. If this seems impossible to us, we and our children must come to realize that Christians have had to learn and endure this for centuries. Even today, in the Middle East, Christians are having to learn how to love and have compassion on their enemies, those who would kill them and their families. We can achieve this in our hearts if we remember that, they are just lost sinners, doing as they feel in their hearts they must, because they are bound in spiritual darkness; often they do not know better, or even think that they are doing righteous service to God to harm us! (see John 16:2) We also must remember that, without the grace of God in our lives, we might very well have turned out as the enemies of God's people ourselves.

2. It means that, when God works in our hearts to sanctify us, we become like Him (thus, His "image." It doesn't mean that we will look like God (for, He has no "looks," He's not physical at all) but we will be like Him in our character.

3. To think that we can earn a right to God's love comes from holding the foolish and wrong belief that our actions can be so righteous that, we impress Him. Which is never true! God is so holy, and even our best actions have sin in them; so that we cannot possibly impress Him and earn His love. Anyone who has ever been loved by God receives that love by grace – and grace means, we do not deserve it, but He treats us far better than we deserve.

*Definition*

## GRACE

---

God's undeserved favor, shown when
He treats sinners not only better than
we deserve, but also with kindness that
is the opposite of what we deserve.

# Chapter 5:
# ERHARD'S ACCOUNT OF THE CONFLICT

1 Why would many Christians in a war initiated by the Pope against Christians, be inclined only to fight defensively and not go on the offensive?

2 Why would Theobold tremble when Erhard spoke to him about the love of Jesus? (page 34)

3 Why would Erhard be so loving and concerned about the welfare of Theobold and his family? (page 35)

## Memory Verse

### Matthew 5:39

"But I say to you, Do not resist the one who is evil. But if anyone slaps you on the right cheek, turn to him the other also." (ESV)

"But I say unto you, That ye resist not evil; but whosoever shall smite thee on thy right cheek, turn to him the other also." (KJV)

1. Most Christians have believed that, when ungodly men take up weapons against Christians to slaughter us, we are never to fight back, but that with Christ we suffer for the faith. Some will not even fight defensively. Others have believed it is permissible to fight defensively (stop them, even shoot them, when they come after us, but do not start attacks against them). It can be difficult to know how far to go; because during times of persecution, we will often see just random violence by wicked men who are out of control, and we may feel obliged to protect our friends and families from actions that do not even seem like persecution, but just hateful and pointless violence. Each of us must do as we feel the Word guides us and as our conscience will allow.

2. Men will sometimes tremble when the gospel of the love of Christ is explained to them, because it is so contrary to the kind of religion they would normally, in their fleshly minds, think of. In this case, he probably also trembled because it was extremely different than his own violent way of life, to think of treating others with the love and kindness of God.

3. Erhard is compelled by Jesus' command to "Do good to those who hate you." This makes us like the God who loved us when we were His enemies!

*Activity*

Think of a way that
you could do good things
for someone who hates you.

# Chapter 6:
## A SECRET REVEALED

1   What is the right view to have of Mary, the mother of Jesus?

2   What does the verse Erik quotes to Theobold on page 40 tell us? (from John 2: "Woman, what have I to do with Thee?"

3   Why did Theobold say on page 41, "Shall the Iron-Hearted become a woman?"

## Memory Verse

### Romans 12:15

"Rejoice with those who rejoice; weep with those who weep." (ESV)

"Rejoice with those who rejoice; mourn with those who mourn." (KJV)

1 She is a very privileged and blessed woman, by the Lord, but she has no power to bless us, nor should she ever be prayed to. She certainly should not be worshipped in any way, and no doubt Mary herself is grieved that people do this!

2 Erik is trying to help Theobold understand that Mary was not infallible or holy, as evidenced by the fact that Jesus corrected her when she was mistaken.

3 Like a lot of foolish men, especially warriors and other strong men, he thought it was not manly to cry. This is demonstrated to be wrong by what follows next in the story, when Matthew explains that even Jesus cried, and that was not unmanly of Him. Further, if you read about wars and armies, it has not been unusual at all for even strong, tough men to cry over the suffering of others.

# Chapter 7: A JOYOUS SURPRISE
## and
# Chapter 8: ENEMIES UNITED

1   Is it likely Theobold and Erhard would have ever met in peaceful circumstances (like Erhard's own home) and become reconciled friends, had they not both been wounded?

2   Have you ever been willing to forgive someone who attacked you? Perhaps you have not been attacked with weapons or even fists, but with words and name-calling. Could you forgive them?

3   When John Huss prayed for his enemies and those who were killing him to be forgiven, who was He imitating?

4   It is gruesome to read of the eyes of Christians being pierced (page 55). Who could forgive such people?

## Memory Verse

### Hebrews 13:3

"Remember those who are in prison, as though in prison with them, and those who are mistreated, since you also are in the body." (ESV)

"Remember them that are in bonds, as bound with them; and them which suffer adversity, as being yourselves also in the body." (KJV)

1   It is not very likely that would have ever happened at all! And do you see then, how this proves how God's ways are often very mysterious and surprising? Because He often brings good outcomes out of evil deeds. They could only have met on a battlefield, and then God uses their very conflict to bring them into conversation about the truth of the gospel, in order to save Theobold's soul!

2   We must all recognize that an unwillingness to forgive others will show that we are not yet forgiven ourselves. No matter how serious the wrongs are that they have done to us!

3   He was imitating Jesus Himself! (See 1 Peter 2:20-23) And also others who followed Christ in this way, such as Stephen (see the story in Acts 7:54-60).

4   Do not fear your children learning that the enemies of Jesus Christ still do horrible things to His people — imprisoning, torturing, and murdering those who believe the gospel. It is often in the news and they will learn of it. We must be aware of it, to pray for them. But as for forgiveness, let us always remember that it is only by the grace of God that we are not worse, and that we must forgive others. And yes, if they do not repent of these things, God will one day judge them and make it right.

## Activities

1   Is there a war battlefield near you that you can visit, in a short drive? Many eastern states live near to a Civil War battlefield, and some out west are near a site where there was a battle between the American army and native American Indians. If you can do so, make a visit there and read all you can about it on the signs and the museum exhibits there.

2   Your family probably knows at least one veteran of a war. Make a visit to this soldier, even if he's a very elderly, and ask him questions about what it was like being a soldier. Find out if he ever met someone from the enemy side in person, on peaceful terms, and what their conversation was like.

3   Write a letter to a veteran of war, thanking him for his service to our country in the terrible times of war.

# WANDERING MAY
## Study Guide

Young May does not want to ever leave Farleigh Village. It has been her comfortable hometown in the country for all the days of her life so far, and the idea of moving into the city just sounds awful. But sometimes the events that seem to have no good side to them at all turn out to be God's plan to bring us a greater blessing than we ever had in mind. She meets a friend who introduces her to the good news about Jesus Christ, the Savior of the world!

# Chapter 1:
# FARLEIGH VILLAGE

1   Imagine a town in which NO one knew the Lord Jesus. Outside of America, all over the world, there are many such towns (and nowadays, probably some towns in America, too). Does it make you want to take the gospel there? Or to just pray someone who preaches the gospel would move there.

2   Some unusual phrases are found on pages 3 and 4:

"the housework had become May's charge." – that is, it was May's responsibility

"And then her mother had closed her eyes forever." – that is, she had died

The "Half-Way public house" is an old name for a bar, where men would meet up after work to drink heavily, often getting very drunk before they went home.

3   Why would they complain about how small their wages are, while they waste some of the money they have on substances that will harm them? (pages 6-7) Have you ever complained about how others are mistreating you, when you treated yourself even worse in other ways?

4   Have you ever had to face a major move, from a place you were happy to be living, to somewhere you did not look forward to or feared you would not like? How did you cope with the decision?

## Memory Verse
### Matthew 11:28

"Come to me, all who labor and are heavy laden, and I will give you rest." (ESV)

"Come unto Me, all ye that labour and are heavy laden, and I will give you rest." (KJV)

## Answers for Chapter 1:

1   Your child should understand that, even though not everyone is called to be a missionary, yet we are all called to do the work of evangelism and witness to people. Some will be sent to spiritually desolate places to take the gospel to them. Others will be called to pray for workers to be sent (see Matthew 9:37-38). But all of us who know the gospel have a duty to at least pray and try to witness.

2   Just for clarification – no question. Maybe ask your child, did he or she already know the meaning of some of those phrases?

3   These are good questions to examine ourselves with. Perhaps you can think of some instances in your own experience that you can share with your child, of times when you complained about something, while you were more at fault than you even thought.

4   There is nothing wrong with being displeased or unhappy with big changes in our life that we would prefer did not happen. But if we complain excessively about them and refuse to be happy, we are not acknowledging that God could have a better plan for us than the one we would make; we are not living by faith. Often, a change that people did not want has turned out to bring about much blessing in their lives. Perhaps your family has experiences like this that you can talk about.

# Chapter 2:
## THE JOURNEY

1  You have probably faced the situation of being given a job or work to do that you did not enjoy, or you were very reluctant to do. But there was no avoiding it – you had to. So how do you make yourself content with this situation? For instance, our boys did not enjoy the chore of cleaning the cat's litter box! They were each very reluctant to do it and probably often hoped that one of the others would do it instead.

2  How well do you adapt to big changes in your life and surroundings?

3  What do you think of Ellen's idea (page 33) that "I suppose people that hasn't done any particular harm goes there." (to heaven)

## Memory Verse

### Isaiah 66:13

"As one whom his mother comforts, so I will I comfort you." (ESV)

"As one whom his mother comforteth, so shall I comfort you." (KJV)

1.  If we are going to please the Lord, it's necessary that we learn to be content in whatever circumstances we are in (Phil. 4:11). We can start to get there by first realizing that we need to rely fully on the grace of God; asking the help of the Holy Spirit; also by accepting also that we do not deserve the happier circumstances we want; and also by accepting the fact that, the different circumstances we find ourselves coming into just might be far better than the ones we wanted.

2.  Discuss this with your child and let them openly express what they find most troubling or trying about big changes. It will differ a lot for different people. If your child does not easily open up about this, talk about how it affects you and expand on the subject starting there. Your own transparency about it may help him to open up about it.

3.  Ellen here expresses the common belief that, nearly everyone goes to heaven except for the people who have committed terrible sins. This is a big mistake, as obviously it would mean that only the most awful sinners go to hell, which is not at all what the Bible teaches.

OBEDIENCE

**Father, I Know That All My Life**     559

*I have learned to be content whatever the circumstances. Phil. 4:11*

1. Fa - ther, I know that all my life is por - tioned out for me:
2. I would not have the rest - less will that hur - ries to and fro,
3. I ask thee for the dai - ly strength, to none that ask de - nied,
4. In ser - vice which thy will ap - points there are no bonds for me;

the chang - es that are sure to come, I do not fear to see:
seek - ing for some great thing to do, or se - cret thing to know;
a mind to blend with out - ward life, while keep - ing at thy side,
my se - cret heart is taught the truth that makes thy chil - dren free:

I ask thee for a pres - ent mind, in - tent on pleas - ing thee.
I would be treat - ed as a child, and guid - ed where I go.
con - tent to fill a lit - tle space, if thou be glo - ri - fied.
a life of self - re - nounc - ing love is one of lib - er - ty.

Anna L. Waring, 1850                           MORWELLHAM 6.6.8.6.8.8.
Charles Steggall, 1826–1905

# Chapter 3:
## MAY'S TOWN HOME

1  So, why does Christ invite us to "come to Me" (Matthew 11:28)?

2  How would you answer May's question on page 40: "Does God mean everybody, or only very good people?"

3  How is the Lord Jesus actually able to bear our griefs, carry our sorrows, and show us love?

## Memory Verse
### Isaiah 53:4

"Surely He has borne our griefs and carried our sorrows; yet we esteemed Him stricken, smitten by God, and afflicted." (ESV)

"Surely He hath borne our griefs, and carried our sorrows; yet we did esteem Him stricken, smitten of God, and afflicted." (KJV)

1. Because the burden of your sin is too much for you to bear, and you cannot live with it. You need to find rest from the labor of trying to justify yourself by works, by going to Him. Only He can save you.

2. We need to tell anyone who believes this that the opposite is true. Not just "very good people" can find rest in Christ, but all sorts of people can come to Him; and in fact, only people who understand that they are sinful will come to Him.

3. Our griefs and sorrows are mostly due to our sins. It makes us sad in some ways when other people sin against us, but the biggest harm to our lives comes from our own sins. He forgives those and shows us love by both forgiving us and changing us from within – saving us from our sins. He saves us from the penalty of our sins, and their power too.

# Chapter 4:
## SOMETHING ABOUT JOY

1 What do we know about God (page 48) that helps us when disappointing changes come into our lives?

2 May wished Jesus was in the world. Would it be easier to come to the Lord Jesus if He was walking on earth, or would it be the same as it is now?

3 Why does the Bible verse quoted on the bottom of page 63 (it's Acts 13:38) speak of Jesus as "a Man?" Is it just as important that He be a Man as that He is God?

## Memory Verse

### 1 Timothy 2:5

"For there is one God, and there is one mediator between God and men, the man Christ Jesus." (ESV)

"For there is one God, and one mediator between God and men, the man Christ Jesus." (KJV)

1　We know that God always knows what is best for us. Sometimes, when life brings us great pain, this can be a hard truth to believe, but even in the worst of times we must hang onto the Lord by faith and trust that it is so.

2　It would actually be harder to follow the Lord Jesus if He was in this world; because then we would have to be where He is (physically). This is why, when He left this world, He taught His disciples that it was better for them that He went away, because then the Holy Spirit would come (John 16:7).

3　Jesus is called "a Man" in that verse, and in the book, because He is in fact God coming in the flesh. This is why He was born to Mary into the human race – to be a perfect substitute for us, by being God and man at the same time. So yes, to save us, it's just as important that He be a man as well as God.

*Activity*

Did you start a thankfulness journal that we suggested a book or two ago? Whether you did or not, write down some things about the Lord Jesus that you are thankful for.

# Chapter 5:
# ELLEN'S STORY

1  How can we ever believe that the Lord Jesus loves us even more than our parents do, as May believes (page 68)?

2  What does Ellen mean by saying May's father is a "rolling stone," who gathers no moss? (page 71)

3  When Ellen says that religious people think they are better than anyone else, and always look miserable, is this true? (bottom of page 71)

4  What showed that Ellen did not really know yet what repenting meant? (pages 79-80)

## Memory Verse

### Proverbs 28:13

"Whoever conceals his transgressions will not prosper, but he who confesses and forsakes them will obtain mercy." (ESV)

"He that covereth his sins shall not prosper: but whoso confesseth and forsaketh them shall have mercy." (KJV)

1   There is no way to see or know this but by faith in the Word of God. The Scriptures tell us it is so, and knowing that they are the Word of God, we are to believe it and can have confidence it is true.

2   It's an old phrase which means that someone does not stay in one place long, and so he does not end up close to any people. He stays a loner.

3   Sadly, for some religious people, it is true. But those who know the Lord truly by grace never think they are better than others; we know we are sinful. And should not ever be miserable either, because we have the joy of the Lord.

4   She admits it herself, in that she is only afraid that God punishes people for their sins, but she is not sorry for doing them. When we have truly repented, we are sorrowful for our sins and we don't want to do them anymore, so as to be pleasing to God.

## Activities

1   Take a drive – on the same day – through a very lovely country region, with nice farmhouses and lands, and then as soon as you can, through a rough and ugly part of the city nearest you. Imagine what it would be like, to have to move from one of these places to the other, when you did not want to!

2   Is there someone you know, who is very sad about their circumstances, and to whom you could witness about Jesus? It could be that you are the one who has the best solution of all to their unhappiness, by sharing with them the joy of eternal life in Christ. Can you begin to pray about someone with whom you could share the good news about Jesus?

# THE WEED WITH AN ILL NAME
## Study Guide

Being little sinners themselves, children are very liable to judge other sinners as worse ones than themselves! We all tend to minimize our own sins and be overly offended at those of others. How much more God-honoring our lives would be, if we hated our own sins as much as much as we detest the sins we see in other people. It is very easy for a child who has been taught a little about the Bible to become a self-righteous Pharisee. During a summer trip to their aunt and uncle's farm, George and Fanny learn the gospel more clearly than ever before, and a lot of self-justifying habits come under the microscope of God's Word and are exposed for the serious problem they are!

# Chapter 1:
# A LETTER

1   So, Fanny is prone to sin by losing her temper, and George is inclined to sinful pride. What does the Bible say about these faults? How dangerous are they?

2   The chapter clearly says that God sent trials into the lives of Mr. & Mrs. Gray, even though they were godly people whose lives were pleasing to Him. Why does God send trials to such people?

3   Parents in our country and modern times do not often lose their children to an early death; but in past centuries (and still today in other, poorer countries) children do die young a lot more often than we experience it in America. How would you be able to endure the death of one of your children?

## Memory Verse

### James 4:6

"God opposes the proud, but He gives grace to the humble." (ESV)

"God resisteth the proud, but giveth grace unto the humble." (KJV)

1  The Proverbs (and many other Scriptures) tell us to beware of a hot-tempered person (Prov. 22:24, 15:18) and that pride goes before a fall (Prov. 16:18); and that God is against the proud (Prov. 16:5, James 4:6).

   Proverbs 22:24: "Make no friendship with a man given to anger, nor go with a wrathful man."

   Proverbs 15:18: "A hot-tempered man stirs up strife, but he who is slow to anger quiets contention."

   Proverbs 16:18: "Pride goes before destruction, and a haughty spirit before a fall."

   Proverbs 16:5: "Everyone who is arrogant in heart is an abomination to the Lord; be assured, he will not go unpunished."

   James 4:6b: "God opposes the proud, but gives grace to the humble."

2  He is committed to make us partakers of His holiness (as the reference to Hebrews 12 describes) and to do that, requires more than only positive influences. It also takes afflictions. After we have suffered them, God's people will often agree with the Psalm (119) quoted on page 3, that it is good for us to have been afflicted. As for Fanny and George, God was intending to root out the sin in the hearts of these children, and their trials did just that!

3  The death of a child is one of the most difficult afflictions anyone can ever experience. But if we accept the truth that life is the gift of God, to give when He wills and to whomever He wills, we realize then that He has the right to make it last as long as He wills and to conclude anyone's life at the time of His choosing. For each of us, and our times, He has His own purpose.

# Chapter 2:
## TWO MORE LETTERS

1    The author of this book makes a point of showing us some obvious differences between George's letter and Fanny's letter. Do you think the writer is being too hard on George?

2    What are the good traits that can be seen in these two children, from their letters?

3    What do you think about the children's letters? Did any other feature of either letter capture your attention or interest, good or bad?

## Memory Verse
### 1 Thessalonians 5:18

"Give thanks in all circumstances; for this is the will of God in Christ Jesus for you." (ESV)

"In every thing give thanks: for this is the will of God in Christ Jesus concerning you." (KJV)

1. The writer is pretty tough on George, and he does show some good traits. Nonetheless, it is true that a great deal of the letter is about him and what makes him happy, and it does contain some complaints about other people which are really not necessary to say.

2. Both George and Fanny do say some complimentary words about other people, noticing their good attributes and expressing thankfulness for those; and they both express hope that their father is getting well.

3. Just enjoy conversing with your child about this, encouraging him to share whatever he has noticed in the letters; after hearing your child's observations, if there are any features you want to point out, follow up with that.

*Activity*

Write a letter to a relative—one of your grandparents, aunts, or uncles, and don't ask them for a thing! Just express your thankfulness for them, something about them that you can sincerely be thankful for. On another occasion, try writing a letter of thanks to your pastor.

# Chapter 3:
# DEVELOPMENTS OF CHARACTER

1    I think almost any reader will see that the way George spoke to Sam was rude, provocative, and uncalled for. For a child to speak to an adult in this way was very wrong. But, would it have been acceptable or reasonable for George to speak to Sam this way, if they were both adults?

2    Why do you suppose Mr. Gray postponed talking to George and Sam, rather than settling the dispute between them right away?

3    Have you ever been caught in the middle of an argument between two friends or two people that you loved? What was it like and were you able to help them reconcile or not? ("Reconciling" is ending the argument and being at peace with one another.)

4    If you were not able to help them reconcile, as you look back, is there a different way you could have helped that might have brought about a better result?

## Memory Verse
### Proverbs 17:14

"The beginning of strife is like letting out water, so quit before the quarrel breaks out." (ESV)

"The beginning of strife is as when one letteth out water: therefore leave off contention, before it be meddled with." (KJV)

1. Absolutely not! George's rudeness to Sam was quite wrong, for a child to be so disrespectful to an adult; but even if he had been an adult, the way he spoke to Sam was rude and provocative. He started an argument with him for no good reason at all, and he made it worse and worse by refusing to listen.

2. Sometimes, it can be a good idea to let people's tempers cool off a bit, and give them time to think before starting to correct them. Certainly, it is often necessary to correct people right away rather than wait; but at other times, it is good judgment to let them settle down a bit and then talk to them. This seems to be what Mr. Gray was thinking.

3. If your child answers that he has found himself in that spot of being caught between friends or family members who are arguing, help him to arrive at an understanding that the best way he can help in such a situation is to not get angry or inflamed himself over the matter, but to keep calm and help them to both calm down too. This is a good occasion to emphasize that we can help others settle their disputes if we are wise from knowing the Word of God. Knowing the Word is ultimately what will help us most to come to correct conclusions about who was right or wrong in a matter.

4. As you work through this question, make sure your child knows that even if he cannot bring other people to be reconciled, that it is not necessarily his or her fault. There are occasions when one person or both are not genuinely trying to be peacemakers, and another person cannot be held at fault for being unable to bring them together. The two disputing have to want peace, too!

# Chapter 4:
# MORE CHARACTER DEVELOPMENT

1    Most of us can relate to George when we read of how, when he knew that he was wrong, he just got angrier instead of humbling himself. When you are angry and feel a desire to justify yourself – but know you are wrong – how do you get control of yourself again so that you can respond the right way?

2    "Feelings! As if those kind of people have feelings," George says on page 25, speaking of Sam. There is much that is very wrong with speaking that way of another person. What would you say are some of the wrongs of it?

3    It is a step in the right direction that George was able to bring himself to apologize to Sam by the end of this chapter; but something about his spirit was still wrong. What does it mean that, he had the wrong attitude about apologizing and was "proud of his humility"? (page 29)

## Memory Verse

### James 3:8-9

"But no human being can tame the tongue. It is a restless evil, full of deadly poison. With it we bless our Lord and Father, and with it we curse people who are made in the likeness of God." (ESV)

"But the tongue can no man tame; it is an unruly evil, full of deadly poison. Therewith bless we God, even the Father; and therewith curse we men, which are made after the similitude of God." (KJV)

## Answers for Chapter 4:

1  It becomes much harder for us to receive correction and reproof when we are angry. One of the most effective ways to get back in the right frame of mind is, to try to think about the future and think about how I will feel later about myself and my actions. This will usually make us realize, I'm not going to be pleased with myself and how I reacted, so I may as well settle down and listen to the correction now.

2  George's talk makes clear that he thinks some people are beneath him, that is, less important or less valuable than he is. This is never true. Every person is the image of God and we should not speak about them as if they have less human dignity than we do.

3  Sin is very multi-sided in all of us. About the time we think we have defeated a certain sin in our lives, often another one is being exposed. It is quite amazing, but true, that once we are aware that people will admire us for being humble, that we might sometimes choose to appear to humble ourselves, in order to be noticed and admired for it!

Two other very helpful books on this subject are *Grace Raymond: The Evil and Cure of a Passionate Temper* (a story to read to children) and *The Heart of Anger: Practical Help for the Prevention and Cure of Anger in Children*, by Lou Priolo (for parents to read). Both of these are available from Grace and Truth Books.

# Chapter 5:
# MORE CHARACTER IS REVEALED

1  George looks down on his teacher, Mr. Paris, because he is a poor man. Why do you suppose some people look down on others for being poor?

2  Page 33 has this humorous remark: "If hot-tempered people waited until they had a good reason to be terribly angry, then they would never be upset." Why is this both humorous and mostly true?

3  What do you think happened between Fanny and Susan?

## Memory Verse

### Ephesians 4:26

"Be angry and do not sin; do not let the sun go down on your anger." (ESV)

"Be ye angry, and sin not: let not the sun go down upon your wrath." (KJV)

## Answers for Chapter 5:

1.   There can be numerous reasons those who have plenty of money look down on the poor. One of the worst is simply because, they feel that poor people do not have to be taken seriously or respected; they have no power anyway. Other reasons are, some assume that those who are poor have not tried hard enough to make an income, or that they are lazy. This is certainly not the case with a man who is a tutor! George should have known better. Almost all teachers have been diligent students of something with their minds. Regardless of the possible reasons, and whatever George's may have been, there are no good reasons to disrespect the poor.

2.   It is humorous because, it's revealing of human nature in a witty way. This shows that the real source of anger in hot-tempered people is themselves. They do not wait for a reason to be angry; they just get angry, whether there is a reason to or not!

  And, it is mostly true because, while there certainly are valid reasons which make people get angry (so we can't really say *never*), yet most of the time, what we get angry about, we do not need to let it provoke us to that response. In other words, nearly all anger is avoidable if we are in control of ourselves.

3.   It is evident that Fanny must have hit Susan on the face. Discuss with your child whether they have ever had occasion to forgive someone who actually physically hit them.

# Chapter 6:
## THE CLOVER FIELD

1  In what way are weeds that harm a garden or farm crops comparable to sins in our lives and hearts?

2  Why do you suppose it is called "The weed with an ill name"? What does the word "ill" mean in this case?

## Memory Verse

### Hebrews 12:15

"See to it that no one fails to obtain the grace of God,
that no root of bitterness springs up and causes trouble,
and by it many become defiled." (ESV)

""Looking diligently lest any man fail of the grace of
God; lest any root of bitterness springing up trouble
you, and thereby many be defiled." (KJV)

1.  For one, the sins of our hearts tend to choke out the growth of good and holy traits in our hearts. Sin also consumes the energy and thought life, so that we cannot focus on growing in righteousness as we ought to. We are too occupied in our minds with our sins.

2.  When we say "ill" nowadays, we normally mean a person who is sick, unhealthy. But this is an older definition of the word "ill" – meaning, disgusting or displeasing.

*Definition*

**RESPECTFULNESS**

Treating others with
honor and esteem.

*from* Kids of Character Bible Study, *by Marilyn Boyer, page 157*

# Chapter 7:
# ANOTHER VISIT TO THE CLOVER FIELD

1   We can see from this story that, it's possible that neglect of your own farm or property can result in doing other people wrong. Our negligence of what is our own can actually be a failure to love others, too. Can you think of any ways in which you can do better at taking care of things you own, in ways that will affect others for good, so they do not suffer harm?

2   What does Mr. Gray mean by using the old saying (page 58) "While the faults of our neighbors with freedom we blame ..."?

## Memory Verse

### Romans 14:7

"For no one of us lives to himself, and none of us dies to himself." (ESV)

"For none of us liveth to himself, and no man dieth to himself." (KJV)

1  A few answers fit here. For instance, if we do not take good care of our cars, it could be a danger to others who ride in them with us. If we have a dead tree near the edge of our property, that could fall on our neighbor's house, that is not thinking lovingly of him or treating him right. To have a mean dog that might bite our neighbors running loose is not doing our neighbors right. And perhaps your own family can think of more ways to apply this that pertain specifically to your home and where you live.

2  He means that, while we blame others "with freedom" (easily, quickly) we do not notice our own sins and faults as much as theirs. Especially theirs which have an effect on us!

# Chapter 8:
## THE LECTURE

1 Maybe your parents and family read books aloud together, as the Gray family did here. How have you found that beneficial?

2 What sort of "field" does Mr. Gray have in mind in the talk he is giving to George and Fanny?

3 Does Mr. Gray mean to accuse especially George & Fanny of having evil hearts, or is he saying that all people by nature and from birth have evil and sinful hearts?

4 Why is George always trying to answer Mr. Gray in a way that escapes the conviction of his points?

5 George clearly changes his tone by the end of the chapter. What do you think led to this?

## Memory Verse

### Proverbs 4:23

"Keep your heart with all vigilance, for from it flow the springs of life." (ESV)

"Keep thy heart with all diligence; for out of it are the issues of life." (KJV)

1   It's such a great way for the family to stop their busyness of the day together, and to enjoy the same thing, which puts all the minds in the household on the same subject. Learning together in a household makes it really stick!

2   He makes clear on page 63, that our hearts are like fields in which something grows – either fruitful crops or worthless weeds.

3   He's very clear that, all people have this problem with sin. Make sure that, when you hear this truth, that you don't choose to be personally offended by it! We all have sin problems and you are no different, so you have no grounds or basis to be annoyed that we talk about it.

4   When a person does this – child or adult – they are trying very hard to avoid being convicted of their own sins.

5   When this happens, the Spirit of God has been at work in someone's heart, and usually using wisdom in someone's words.

# Chapter 9:
# THE CONFESSION

1  Even though Fanny was able to control her words from exploding out into what appeared to be a burst of hot temper, what made her conclude that she still had a life full of sinful weeds?

2  What are the different outcomes for us, according to 1 John 1:9 (page 82) if we say that we have no sin or if we confess and admit our sins?

3  Can we take comfort from the fact that God knows our sins, or should we find it a frightening or terrifying thought?

## Memory Verse

### Proverbs 28:13

"Whoever conceals his transgressions will not prosper; but he who confesses and forsakes them will obtain mercy." (ESV)

"He that covereth his sins shall not prosper; but whoso confesseth and forsaketh them shall have mercy." (KJV)

1  It was that there were still angry and bitter thoughts in her heart. Even if we can subdue angry words from coming out, if we find that we still have angry and bitter thoughts, it shows that sin is powerful within us.

2  The one results in us being self-deceived and showing that there is no truth in us. The other results in God forgiving us! Because we are facing the truth honestly, before people and Him.

3  The answer to that all depends on whether we are admitting our sins to Him or concealing them and acting as if we didn't do them. If we are confessing our sins to God, then we can have peace as we know that He is aware of them all; He will not judge those who confess their sins to Him. But if we are hiding our sins, we have much reason to fear His judgment. For God hates the ways of all who try to conceal their sins.

# Chapter 10:
# THE RINGDOVE

1 What made Fanny merciful towards the boy who had harmed her by shooting her bird?

2 Why did teasing Fanny no longer "work," as George said? (page 94)

## Memory Verse

**Psalm 51:10**

"Create in me a clean heart, O God, and renew a right spirit within me." (ESV)

"Create in me a clean heart, O God, and renew a right spirit within me." (KJV)

1   She was now aware of her own sins, and reluctant to judge others harshly for theirs. Once you know that you also sin in a lot of ways, you become more careful not to judge the motives or actions of others too harshly.

2   Because, having become a Christian, Fanny was no longer easily offended.

## Activity

Look at "the fruit of the Spirit" as found in Galatians 5:22 (below). Talk about each of these, one by one — what are the results of each of them, in family life?

"But the fruit of the Spirit is love, joy, peace, patience, kindness, goodness, faithfulness, gentleness, self-control; against such things there is no law."

# Chapter 11:
## GOOD SEEDS SPRING UP

1  When George was willing to confess to pride, and his uncle indicated that there would still be more sins to be found in his heart, why was George upset and felt his uncle was making fun of him?

2  Page 103 says that Fanny's natural tendencies (to sin) did not completely change, but were easier to control. Why doesn't Jesus totally free us from our tendencies to sin in this life?

3  George's closing letter shows that the way we interpret correction and rebuke from others, about our sins, mostly depends on us and what sort of heart we have. Describe the transformation in George's heart in your own words.

## Memory Verse

### Psalm 141:5

"Let a righteous man strike me — it is a kindness.  Let him rebuke me — it is oil for my head; let my head not refuse it." (ESV)

"Let the righteous smite me; it shall be a kindness: and let him reprove me, it shall be an excellent oil, which shall not break my head." (KJV)

1   Too often, when people have the sin in their lives pointed out, they feel that the person doing so is against them or mocking them. Don't ever feel this way, it's not necessary. We all have a lot of sin to change and should not find it challenging or vexing when someone says so. Rather, it is a kindness to us, a gesture of love, and we should see it as such.

2   We don't fully know the answer to this, but it's probably because we are still in a world with other sinners, and He wants us to be able to show compassion to them, and not elevate ourselves above them in our thoughts; and so He will not finally and completely deliver us from our sins in this life, but will do so in the life to come in heaven.

3   Let your child speak on this and describe what he thinks about the transformation in George's heart. After you listen, make sure he or she understands that such a change is:

a) the work of the Holy Spirit

b) requires accepting conviction of our own sin

c) and comes from receiving God's Word into our hearts and knowing Jesus Christ as our Lord and Savior.

# Activities

1   Can you find a place in your yard or garden, where some weeds are choking the life out of some useful and desirable plants that you would rather see thriving there? Take a good look at them and notice the damage they do and hindrance they are! Then pull them out!

2   Can you think of anyone poor you know, or you have seen, who people might be likely to despise or look down on? Try taking that person some food and having a conversation with them. You might be surprised at learning how they ended up in that spot. It may or may not have been their own fault; but if you listen with thoughtfulness and care, you'll recognize that, except for the grace of God in your life, you and your family could have ended up there too!